THE ASSOCIATED PRESS PICTORIAL HISTORY OF

BASEBALL

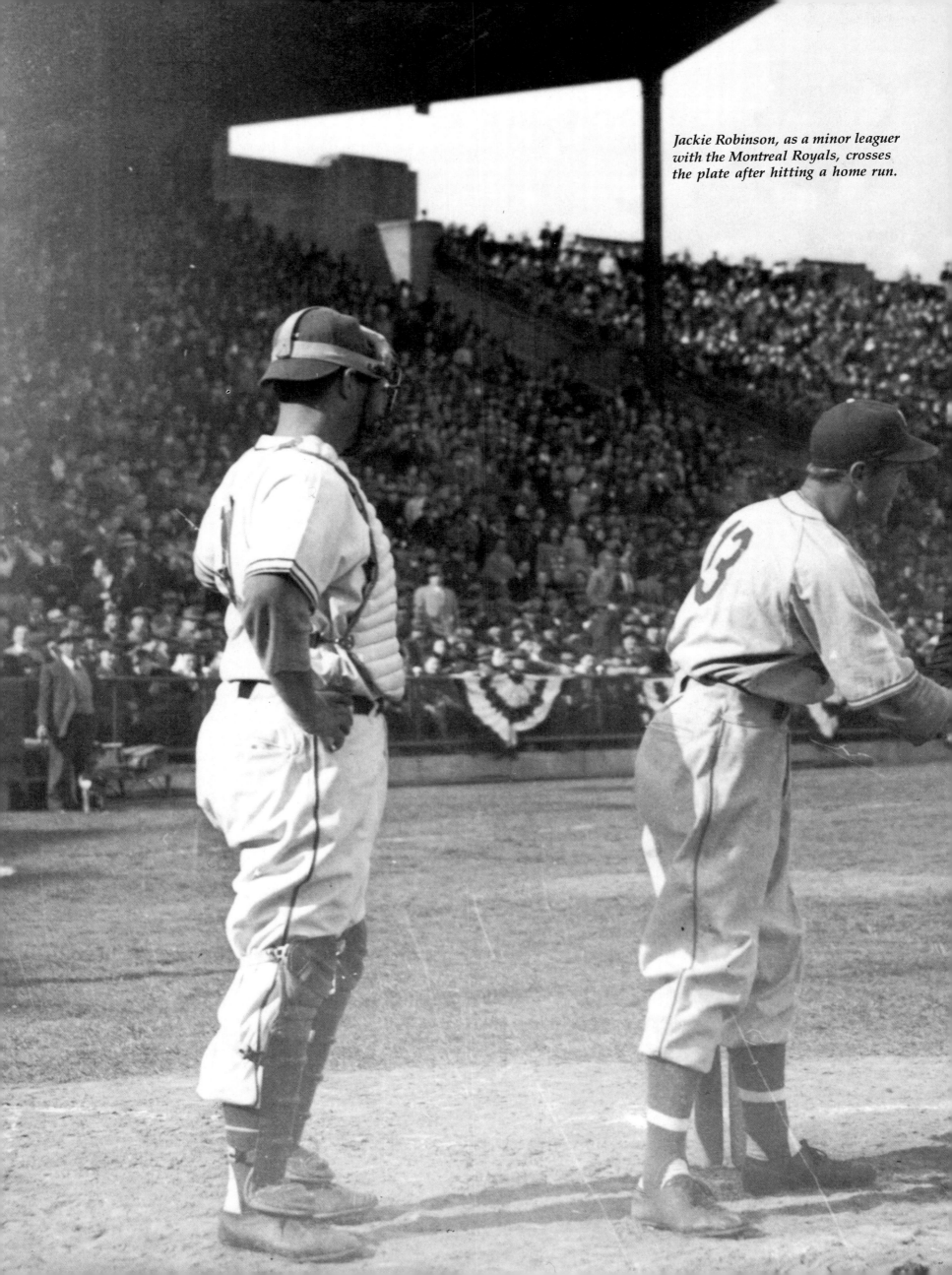

Jackie Robinson, as a minor leaguer with the Montreal Royals, crosses the plate after hitting a home run.

THE ASSOCIATED PRESS PICTORIAL HISTORY OF

BASEBALL

by
HAL BOCK

JG PRESS

Revised Edition

FOR FRAN

As all things are.
Her spirit of scientific inquiry
always led her to wonder about
''the ancient Heinie Manush.''

ACKNOWLEDGMENT

Assembling a book that covers 150 years or so of baseball history was a labor of love but no simple task. The job was made possible by what has gone before, great reference works that are cornerstones in the literature of the sport. They include *The Baseball Encyclopedia*, *The Baseball Hall of Fame 50th Anniversary Book* by Gerald Astor, *The Illustrated History of the National League* and its companion *American League* by Donald Honig, *The World Series Complete Play-by-Play*, compiled by Richard M. Cohen and David S. Neft, *The New York Times Sports Encyclopedia*, *The Sporting News Complete Baseball Record Book*, and *All-Star Baseball Since 1933* by Robert Obojski and *The Hall of Fame Gallery* by Martin Appel and Burt Goldblatt. Each contributed mightily to this volume.

Revised edition

Editor: Norm Goldstein
Photo Researcher: Marc Seigerman

Design by Combined Books, Inc.
26 Summit Grove Avenue, Suite 207
Bryn Mawr, PA 19010

Produced by Wieser & Wieser, Inc.
118 East 25th Street
New York, NY 10010

Published by
World Publications, Inc.
455 Somerset Avenue
North Dighton, MA 02764

ISBN 0-9640034-1-4

Printed in Spain

CONTENTS

FIRST INNING

IN THE BEGINNING 1900–1910

Baseball as we know it was born when a former sports writer, Ben Johnson, dreamed of a confederation to rival the National League, begun in 1876.

As America headed for the turn of the century, Johnson moved slowly but surely in that direction. He began with the Western League, which included among its Midwestern franchises a team in St. Paul, Minnesota. The team was operated by Charles Comiskey, a former first baseman in the old American Association and ex-manager of the Cincinnati club. Johnson and Comiskey spent considerable time together solving the problems of the world and contemplating the future of baseball which, for them, included a new major league to compete with the established National League.

By 1900, Johnson and Comiskey were ready to roll. They changed the Western League's name to the American League and asked the National League for recognition. The National, less than thrilled to have company on baseball's block, simply ignored the interlopers. The American League went ahead anyway, playing mostly in Western League cities in 1900. A year later, Johnson was back, proposing to add Eastern cities to his league.

The East was the National League's bailiwick so it seemed logical to request a meeting. The National League agreed and when Johnson showed up, he was asked to wait outside a conference room. While he cooled his heels, the National League executives conducted their business and then disappeared out a side entrance.

Enraged by that cavalier treatment, Johnson moved unilaterally, essentially declaring war by installing franchises in Chicago, Boston, and Philadelphia, all of which already had National League franchises. Detroit, Baltimore, Washington, Cleveland and Milwaukee completed the AL lineup for its first season, 1901.

Franchises are one thing. Stocking them with quality players is quite another and Johnson knew that unless he could entice the best athletes to play in his new league, the venture would have trouble succeeding. He also knew where to find the players he wanted—in the rival National League. And, the reserve clause notwithstanding, he went right after them.

The National League had a $2,400 salary ceiling for its players and when it became obvious that Johnson's American League would ignore that barrier, top names

Adrian "Cap" Anson played 22 seasons for Chicago of the National League and became the first player to amass 3,000 career hits.

Ban Johnson, recognizing the market for another baseball league, organized the American League with eight teams in 1901.

started moving. Among the early emigres were pitcher Cy Young, who left St. Louis for Boston, pitcher Joe McGinnity, who went from Brooklyn to Baltimore, and infielder John McGraw, who left St. Louis for Baltimore. Then there were infielders Jimmy Collins and Nap Lajoie, who not only jumped to the new league but compounded their departures by remaining in the cities in which they had been playing, Collins in Boston and Lajoie in Philadelphia. The National League was naturally outraged and, in the case of Lajoie, his old team, the Phillies, got an injunction preventing him from playing for his new club, the Athletics. Lajoie led the new league in hitting with a .422 batting average in 1901 but then, unwilling to test the court order, simply switched to Cleveland the next year. The team was so thrilled to have him, it adopted his name, the Naps.

Lajoie starred for Cleveland in seven cities but when the Naps went into Philadelphia, he retreated over the state line, not wishing to challenge the law. That law, however, applied only in Pennsylvania where the courts had ruled in favor of the reserve clause. Elsewhere, the clause, which tied a player to his team until he was traded, sold or released, did not fare as well and players moved freely. The exodus was substantial. Familiar names like shortstop Bobby Wallace, outfielders Ed Delahanty and Wee Willie Keeler and pitchers Jack

Chesbro and Wild Bill Donovan made the switch.

What's more, Johnson had substantial people in charge of the American League franchises. Four of the eight managers in the league's inaugural season—Collins in Boston, McGraw in Baltimore, Clark Griffith in Chicago and Connie Mack in Philadelphia—would wind up in the Hall of Fame. So would Young, who would win 511 games and Lajoie, whose .422 batting average in that first season set a standard never topped in the AL.

Griffith, doubling as pitcher, won 24 games and led Chicago to the pennant. Like the city's National League representative, which won that league's first race, it was an accomplishment by the franchise that would be repeated only occasionally in future years. Young led the league with 33 wins for Boston. Mack's Athletics, even with Lajoie's astounding .422 season, finished fourth behind Detroit. Iron Man McGinnity pitched in 48 games for Baltimore, but McGraw's team finished fifth as Washington and Cleveland brought up the rear.

Just as Johnson's American League lured talent, the National League fought back. McGraw's feisty reputation made him an early target for the new league but his constant bickering with umpires and Johnson's steadfast defense of them soon put the manager of the Orioles and the league president on a collision course. Midway through the 1902 season, the split became permanent and McGraw departed Baltimore for New York, to become manager of the Giants. He brought four players with him, most notably McGinnity and catcher Roger Bresnahan.

When he got to New York, McGraw examined the 23-man roster and immediately crossed off 11 names. "I can finish last just as easily with 12 men as with 23," he said. Owner Andrew Freedman was thrilled with his new manager's penurious approach to his task and the fact that the Giants finished last hardly disturbed management. Of more concern than the standings to Freedman and the other owners were the attendance figures for the rival leagues. The National League's 1,684,000 suffered by comparison to the American League's 2,228,000. And in each of the four cities where the leagues were in direct competition—Boston, Chicago, Philadelphia and St. Louis—the American League had the better numbers. Clearly some accommodation would have to be made.

At first, the National League tried offering to take in four of the American League teams to form a single 12-team league. Johnson was not interested and eventually an agreement was hammered out maintaining a separate but equal status for the two leagues. There would be no more raiding of the other league's talent. Rules would be standardized and schedules would be drawn up together to avoid conflicts. The reserve clause, an integral part of roster stability, would be respected. In other words, peace had broken out. But the old wounds were slow to heal on some fronts and in August, with Pittsburgh comfortably in front of the National League and Boston enjoying a big lead in the American, Barney Dreyfuss, owner of the Pirates, decided to spice up the summer. He challenged Boston to a postseason series, a showdown between the leagues.

Henry Killilea, Boston's owner, was intrigued by the challenge and relayed it to Johnson. Nothing went on in the league without the president's approval and Johnson, recognizing the opportunity such a showdown would afford his fledgling league, gave Boston the green light, with one admonition. "You must beat them," he advised Killilea.

The series was set as the best-of-nine games and offered an intriguing matchup. Both teams had player-managers who would wind up in the Hall of Fame—Jimmy Collins with Boston and Fred Clarke with Pittsburgh. Collins' pitching staff was anchored by Cy Young, who had won 28 games that season, while the Pirates had one of the National League's very best players, shortstop Honus Wagner. The series began rather embarrassingly for Boston and Young, who was tagged for four runs in the top of the first inning. That was plenty of support for Deacon Phillippe, a 24-game winner during the regular season, who went all the way in a 7–3 victory. Pittsburgh outfielder Jimmy Sebring had the distinction of hitting the first World Series home run.

Bill Dinneen got Boston even with a 3–0 shutout in Game Two but Phillippe, pitching on just one day's rest, won Game Three, 4–2. A travel day and a rainout enabled Pittsburgh to start Phillippe again in Game Four and again he won, this time 5–4 as a late Boston rally fell short. It was, however, the last game the Pirates would win.

Honus Wagner, a Pittsburgh Pirates shortstop, had 17 consecutive .300 seasons, including eight as National League batting champion.

Nap Lajoie

Cy Young won Game Five 11–2 and Dinneen evened the Series with a 6–3 victory. Phillippe, pitching with the luxury of three days of rest, went after the clincher in Game Seven but was beaten by Young, 7–3. Now, with Pittsburgh in trouble, Clarke came right back to Phillippe and he responded with his fifth complete game. But Dinneen pitched a shutout and Boston had won the Series, delivering on Ban Johnson's ultimatum.

How significant was this first showdown between the leagues? From an economic standpoint, the event was rather modest. A fan could buy a ticket for $1.50 and the payoff for the players was an extra two weeks of pay plus a piece of the gate receipts. From the leagues' standpoint, however, it was dramatic. Egos were involved and the cast of characters in those days had an ample supply of that particular commodity. The National League was embarrassed by losing to Johnson's upstarts and a year later when McGraw's Giants rode the strong arms of Joe McGinnity and Christy Mathewson to the NL pennant, the manager made sure there would be no tainting his title. He simply refused to risk his team's accomplishment in any postseason series. The Giants would not play Boston, which had won the AL title again. It was McGraw's way of getting even with Ban Johnson, with whom he had quarreled frequently when the feisty manager had been in Baltimore. What's more, McGraw's boss, John T. Brush, was not thrilled with Johnson's decision to place an AL franchise in New York to compete with the Giants. So, in 1904, there would be no World Series.

Although McGraw and Brush believed they had good and proper reasons for snubbing the upstarts from the American League, the public was less than enthused about the Giants' decision. Also unhappy were the other National League owners, who recognized the promotional possibilities a postseason series offered. By 1905, even Brush was convinced and it was, in fact, the Giants' owner who suggested the best-of-seven format. McGraw's Giants would beat Connie Mack's Philadelphia Athletics in five games—each of them a shutout. Mathewson started three times for New York, allowing just 14 hits in 27 innings. McGinnity had the other shutout for the Giants and the only Philadelphia victory went to Chief Bender, who shut the Giants out in Game Two.

Mathewson was at the top of his game in 1905, after his third straight 30-win season for the Giants. He befuddled hitters with a pitch he called a reverse curve or a fadeaway, essentially the forerunner of the modern screwball. It helped him win 20 games in his first full major league season, even though he was pitching for a dreadful Giants team that finished next to last and won just 52 games all year. In 1903, he was 30–13 and then won 33 and 31 games the next two seasons. More than his production on the field, however, Mathewson's image off it proved vital to baseball.

At the turn of the century, ballplayers were considered a rather scruffy community. They were mostly crude, uneducated men, who were frowned upon rather than respected. Mathewson, however, was neither crude nor uneducated. He came from a respected family and was the president of his class at Bucknell University where he played baseball, basketball and football. The word was that he neither drank nor smoked and he became an instant hero in a game that desperately needed image-building. It was ironic that Mathewson found himself pitching for McGraw, a product of Baltimore's bare-knuckle champions of the 1890s, who played the game with reckless abandon, asking no quarter and certainly giving none. Typical of the Orioles' style is a story told about the second major league at-bat of Honus Wagner, who would become one of the most magnificent players of his time. Wagner tagged a pitch between outfielders and it seemed a sure three-base hit. As he rounded first, he ran into a textbook hip check by Jack Doyle. Hughie Jennings blocked his path at second, sending him on a wide route there. By the time he got to third, McGraw had the ball waiting for a not-so gentle tag to the midsection that left the rookie gasping for breath.

To Wagner's credit, he learned his lesson. The next time around the bases, he decked Doyle and Jennings and steamrolled into McGraw. He was in the majors to stay, and rightfully so. He would bat .344 that season, starting a string of 17 consecutive .300 seasons, including eight as NL batting champion. He also led the league in steals six times.

Wagner and Mathewson were the top players in the National League, but they were by no means alone. Brooklyn, for example, had Wee Willie Keeler, undersized at 5-foot-4 and barely 140 pounds, who nevertheless would bat .345 for his career, fifth on the all-time list. His simple creed at the plate became one of baseball's most quoted lines.

"I hit 'em where they ain't," Keeler explained.

Keeler once hit in 44 consecutive games, establishing a National League record that lasted 81 years. He also excelled at a new fangled ploy called the hit and run, driving opponents to such distraction that they tried, unsuccessfully, to have it ruled illegal.

Chicago assembled an infield that included shortstop Joe Tinker, second baseman Johnny Evers and first baseman Frank Chance, a trio that would be immortalized by columnist Franklin P. Adams, who paid tribute to

Joe Tinker, in 1914, as player-manager for the Chicago team in the Federal League.

Johnny Evers was the second baseman in baseball's most heralded double play combination.

Walter ''Big Train'' Johnson won 416 games and struck out 3,508 batters during his illustrious career.

their double play prowess, writing:

"These are the saddest of possible words,
"Tinker to Evers to Chance.
"Trio of bear cubs and fleeter than birds,
"Tinker to Evers to Chance.
"Thoughtlessly pricking our gonfalon bubble,
"Making a Giant hit into a double.

"Words that are weighty with nothing but trouble,
"Tinker to Evers to Chance."

In 1908, Adams' words proved prophetic, although not because of a trademark double play. Instead, it was a heads-up play by Evers that changed the result of the pennant race. And the victims, as in Adams' poem, were the Giants.

The double play trio of Tinker-to-Evers-to-Chance included Cubs first baseman Frank Chance.

Three weeks later, with the pennant race coming down the stretch, O'Day was behind the plate for a Cubs-Giants game. The score was 1–1 in the bottom of the ninth and New York had Moose McCormick on third and a 19-year-old rookie named Fred Merkle on first with two out. Al Bridwell singled and as McCormick trotted home, Merkle, following tradition, veered off the field. Evers called for the ball and stepped on second. O'Day ruled Merkle out, but by then the field had been overrun by celebrating fans. There was no way to continue and the game was ruled a 1–1 tie, to be replayed if necessary at season's end. When the Cubs and Giants finished tied for the pennant, the teams played the game over and Chicago won 4–2 to clinch a third straight pennant.

Merkle would spend 16 years in the majors and bat a credible .273. He would be remembered forever, however, for that rookie mistake that came to be known as Merkle's boner.

Two weeks before Merkle's mistake, which was described less than charitably by *The New York Times* as "considerable stupidity," the Washington Senators came into New York for a four-game series against the Yankees. It began on Friday, September 4, with Walter Johnson pitching a six-hitter and winning, 3–0. On Saturday, the 21-year-old right-hander was back, allowing just four hits in a 6–0 victory. And on Monday, in the first game of a doubleheader, Johnson allowed just two hits, winning 4–0, completing a remarkable stretch of three shutouts in four days. And what about Sunday? Law prohibited games on Sunday in New York

Johnny Evers

In early September, the Cubs and Pittsburgh were in the 10th inning of a scoreless tie. The Pirates loaded the bases with two out and when Chief Wilson singled, the runner from third trotted home with the winning run. Following the custom of the day, whenever the game's winning run scored, the other runners would simply head for the clubhouse. Evers considered the situation, called for the ball and touched second base, claiming a force out, the third out of the inning which would nullify the run. Umpire Hank O'Day turned down the appeal, saying he was watching the runner from third and could not tell if Warren Gill, the man on first, had failed to touch second. O'Day was, however, impressed by Tinker's ingenuity and vowed to watch for the play in the future.

then.

And while Johnson was signalling the start of one of baseball's most remarkable pitching careers—he would win 416 games and strike out 3,508 batters—Cy Young was nearing the end of just as great a lifetime on the mound. Young pitched the third no-hitter of his career during the summer of '08 and won 21 games for Boston. He would win 19 the next season in Cleveland and then just 14 more the next two years to finish with 511 victories for 22 seasons. That is 95 more than Johnson, who is second on the all-time list. It is almost certainly the safest record in baseball.

In the summer of 1905, Detroit introduced a young outfielder from Georgia who made a less-than impressive major league debut, batting just .240 in 41 games. It was hardly a sign of things to come because before he was through, Ty Cobb would stamp himself as the most proficient hitter in the history of baseball.

As a rookie, Cobb was an unpopular player.

He did not respond well to the standard pranks the veterans played on him and was a loner with few if any friends. On the field, he compounded his image, sliding into bases with his spikes high. He played the game with an anger for the other team, sometimes for his own team. That could not, however, diminish his production. In his second season, he batted .320, the first of 23 straight years in which he would hit .320 or more. He won 12 batting titles, nine of them consecutively, and his record of 4,191 hits lasted until 1985 when Pete Rose passed him.

Three times, Cobb batted over .400 and his career batting average of .367 is the best in major league history.

Cobb had celebrated battles with a variety of opponents. There is an often-embellished story of the 1909 World Series against Pittsburgh when, standing on first base, he taunted Honus Wagner, stationed at shortstop. Wagner, a veteran of the Oriole wars, is said to have responded by tagging Cobb in the mouth, splitting the Tiger star's lip. That same season, Cobb had slashed Philadelphia third baseman Frank "Home Run" Baker with his spikes.

How hated was Cobb? Consider the 1910 batting race, which came down to the final day with Nap Lajoie chasing Cobb for the crown. This was no small bit of business because the winner would get a shiny new Chalmers automobile to salute the accomplishment.

Cobb had won three straight batting titles, making no friends along the way. He reached the final day of the 1910 season batting .385, decided that was sufficient, and sat out the season's final game. Lajoie, meanwhile, had a doubleheader with Cleveland against St. Louis. The Browns, buried in last place, had a rooting interest in the batting race and it wasn't Cobb. Reportedly, St. Louis manager Jack O'Connor instructed rookie third baseman Johnny Corriden to play deep for Lajoie. This was not a bad strategy, considering Lajoie's reputation as a line drive hitter. In the Cleveland star's first at-bat, he drove a triple. In his next three swings, however, he dropped bunt singles in front of Corriden. In the second game, Lajoie kept up the short ball strategy, bunting on each of his first four at-bats. Three times he beat them out for hits. The other time, Corriden fumbled the ball and it was scored a sacrifice. Lajoie finished the day with a line single, completing an 8-for-8

Christy Mathewson had three consecutive 30-win seasons pitching for the New York Giants in the early part of the century. He relied on a reverse curve, or "fadeaway," the forerunner of the modern screwball.

Christy Mathewson at bat.

day that left him at .384, still short of Cobb's .385.

Chalmers awarded automobiles to both men but Ban Johnson was not amused and conducted an investigation. Corriden was absolved but O'Connor was dismissed. It was never clear whether that was because of the strategy that helped Lajoie or just because the Browns had finished the season 57 games behind first place Philadelphia.

SECOND INNING

2

WAR AND SCANDAL 1911–1918

Nap Lajoie's bunting strategy on the final day of the 1910 season and the apparent encouragement St. Louis manager Jack O'Connor supplied for it must have enraged Ty Cobb.

It didn't take much to get the Georgia Peach seething and the batting title plot was more than sufficient. He wasn't even soothed by the fancy new Chalmers automobile. He would get his revenge on the field.

Cobb came out smoking the next season. He led the league in just about every hitting department, batting a career-high .420, just two points short of Lajoie's record. He had 248 hits, 47 doubles, 24 triples, 83 stolen bases, 144 runs batted in, a .621 slugging percentage and 367 total bases. His 8 home runs, however, were only second best. The winner of the long ball derby in celebration of the end of the dead ball era was Frank Baker of the Philadelphia Athletics, who slammed 11 out of sight. When he hit two more in the World Series against the New York Giants—a mighty feat, indeed—he was awarded a magic nickname. From then on, he was Home Run Baker.

Ty Cobb, ''The Georgia Peach,'' began his career with the Detroit Tigers in 1907. His .367 career batting average is the best in baseball history.

Connie Mack was into nicknames, too. With Baker at third, Stuffy McInnis at first and Eddie Collins and Jack Barry stationed at second base and shortstop, Mack was so impressed that he began calling the group ''The $100,000 Infield.''

Now $100,000 amounts to little more than petty cash in today's baseball economy but in the sport's horse and buggy era, it was a considerable piece of change. The price might have been a trifle inflated, though. Only Baker and Collins would make it to the Hall of Fame while Barry and McInnis had rather ordinary careers. But Mack's nickname bought the quartet considerable attention, much the way Franklin P. Adams' ode to Joe Tinker, Johnny Evers and Frank Chance had done for the three Chicago Cub infielders. Despite Adams' poetry, in the nine years that Tinker, Evers and Chance played together, they never led the league in double plays. But then, in the same year they started calling the Athletics' third baseman Home Run Baker, six National League players hit more than he did. They were led by Wildfire Schulte, who hit 21. Nobody ever called him Home Run Schulte, but that may be because he already had a pretty nifty nickname.

The same might be said for Mordecai Brown, who lost half of his index finger and tore up his thumb and middle finger in a farming accident. The injury became a benefit when Brown started pitching. His sinker zipped this way and that and his curve behaved differently, too. Three Finger Brown was a major problem for hitters and for six straight seasons through 1911, he won 20 or more games.

Twenty wins has always been a notable achievement, but pitchers in baseball's early days often produced more than that. In 1911, for example, 15 pitchers in the two major league won 20 or more. None, however, won more than the 28 registered by rookie Grover Alexander of the Philadelphia Phillies. Alex had seven shutouts that season, four of them in a row, and pitched 31 complete games. It was an impressive debut, especially after it seemed his career might be over following a baseline injury two years before. While running toward second base, he was hit in the head by a throw and remained unconscious for 56 hours. He overcame subsequent double vision and epilepsy problems to become one of baseball's very best pitchers over the next two decades.

Two of the 20-game winners that season pitched for the Giants. Christy Mathewson was a regular member of the 20-win club, surpassing the figure 13 times in his brilliant career. He was joined that season by a newcomer, Rube Marquard, who had been discovered pitching for an ice cream company's factory team. When he won 28 games and struck out 250 batters in the American Association, it triggered a bidding war, unusual for those times. Finally the price was set at an outrageous $11,000, the money going not to Marquard but to his minor league club at Indianapolis. When the youngster struggled in his first two years, critics called him "The $11,000 Lemon." But he began wiping out the sour taste with a 24–7 record in 1911. And the next year he was even better.

From April 11 through July 3, 1912, Marquard won 19 consecutive games. He allowed just 49 runs over the stretch and, in fact, the record would have been 20 straight wins under later rules because he entered one game with the Giants behind and when they rallied to win, the victory was credited to Jeff Tesreau.

Marquard would win 201 games in a Hall of Fame career but discovered how fickle the game can be. Two years after he had won 19 in a row, he lost 12 straight.

While Marquard and Mathewson were pitching the Giants to another pennant, Boston celebrated the opening of Fenway Park by taking the American League flag. The wheelhouse of the Red Sox' effort was Smoky Joe Wood, who won 34 games, 10 of them on shutouts. He had a 1.91 earned run average in the first season that the measure was used to gauge a pitcher's efficiency. Tris Speaker, who had 222 hits including a league-leading 53 doubles, and Duffy Lewis, who drove in 109 runs keyed the Red Sox attack. In the World Series, Boston led three games to one before New York came back to win Games Five and Six, the latter against Wood, the Red Sox ace. The seventh game was tied 1–1 after nine innings, prolonging the drama. In the 10th inning, Merkle singled home the go-ahead run for the

Giants. New York was three outs away from the world championship. It was a goal the Giants never quite reached, though.

With Mathewson on the mound, pinch hitter Clyde Engle led off with a lazy fly ball to center field. Fred Snodgrass lined the ball up, settled comfortably under it and then dropped it for a two-base error. After Harry Hooper flied out, Steve Yerkes walked. Now with the tying and winning runs on base, the dangerous Speaker was at the plate. Mathewson got him to pop up in foul territory outside of first base. Amazingly, Merkle never moved from his position to pursue the ball and catcher Chief Meyers' belated dash was too late. Given a second chance, Speaker singled Engle home with the tying run and after Lewis was intentionally walked, Larry Gardner's long fly brought Yerkes home with the Series winner.

Merkle, the goat of the pennant race loss to Chicago five years earlier on a base running blunder, was wearing horns again. But this time, he had company from Snodgrass, whose error became known as "The $30,000 Muff"—the figure representing the World Series winners' share that the Giants did not collect.

Although disappointed, of course, the loss did not deter the Giants, who won their third straight pennant the next year and did it with Merkle still at first base and Snodgrass still in center field. John McGraw apparently did not hold grudges, at least not with his own players. If you played for the other guys, though, look out. Muggsy McGraw was a tough customer, a carryover from his take-no-guff days with the old Orioles.

Christy Mathewson's achievements pitching for the New York Giants and Cincinnati Reds earned him a place in baseball's Hall of Fame.

Walter Johnson (left) and Ty Cobb.

Meanwhile, although he was unable to singlehandedly lift Washington into that ultimate baseball showcase of the World Series, Walter Johnson was assembling some rather astounding numbers for the otherwise hapless Senators. He won 32 games in 1912, including 16 in a row, then came back with 36 victories in 1913 when he struck out 243 batters, threw 12 shutouts and had a 56-inning scoreless streak. He threw five one-hitters that season as his team finished second for the second year in a row. That was not bad for the franchise that was the butt of jokes like "Washington: First in War, First in Peace, And Last in the American League."

With baseball flourishing, it occurred to some entrepreneurs that there was no reason to limit the game to the American League and National League. When the promoters inquired discreetly about winning approval of the incumbents, they were summarily dismissed by Ban Johnson, much as he had done years before. "There is no room for three major leagues," Johnson told organizers of the Federal League, whereupon they made room.

The Federals established franchises in eight cities—Brooklyn, Baltimore, Buffalo, Chicago, Indianapolis, Kansas City, Pittsburgh and St. Louis—declared the reserve clause null and void and started raiding rosters of AL and NL teams. Three Finger Brown and Joe Tinker of the Cubs, and pitchers Eddie Plank and Chief

Pitcher Cy Young won 511 games in his career. His win total is the highest of all pitchers.

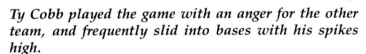

Ty Cobb played the game with an anger for the other team, and frequently slid into bases with his spikes high.

Bender of the Athletics were among the more notable defectors. Walter Johnson was supposed to be going, too, lured by a $10,000 signing bonus offered by the Fed's Chicago franchise. The money was more than Washington boss Clark Griffith could match. But Griffith, a sly operator, was not about to surrender Johnson without a fight. So he approached White Sox owner Charles Comiskey and persuaded him that having Johnson pitching in Chicago for the other league would put a substantial dent in the Sox attendance. Comiskey came up with the bonus money and Johnson stayed in Washington.

When the raids were over, the Federal League had attracted 81 major league players and all manner of legal actions by the American and National Leagues. Ban Johnson was determined to bury the interlopers but the Feds were tenacious. One of their ploys—and one that would be followed by a number of new leagues in other sports for years to come—was to file an antitrust suit against the two major leagues. The federal judge assigned to the case sat in Chicago and deliberated carefully over the merits of the case. He never rendered a decision because before he could, peace broke out between the leagues. However, Kenesaw Mountain Landis, the judge in the case, would be heard from later.

Ban Johnson's dismissal of the Federal League—he called the newcomers "a bunch of bushers"—apparently was shared by the public. Attendance was slim and the court battles had depleted the league's cash reserves. After two years, a settlement was reached and for a league that seemed to be struggling, the terms were pretty good for the Feds.

Contracts of Federal League players were sold to the highest bidders and two major league franchises, the Chicago Cubs and St. Louis Browns, were sold to Federal League owners. Players who had jumped to the new league were welcomed back as the major league teams who had pledged a permanent ban as punishment, simply looked the other way. The Federal League experiment had lasted two years.

In 1913, the Cubs broke up Franklin Adams' favorite double play combination. First baseman Frank Chance, who had doubled as the team's manager, was released and moved to the New York Yankees. Shortstop Joe Tinker was traded to Cincinnati before moving on to the Federal League, and second baseman Johnny Evers, the hero—or villain—of the Merkle boner affair, lasted one more season in Chicago before moving on to Boston, where he participated in one of the greatest comebacks in baseball history.

George Stallings was the manager of the Braves, his fourth major league stop after previous short terms with Philadelphia in the National League and Detroit and New York in the American. His playing career consisted of 20 big league at-bats in seven games spread over three seasons and, until 1914, his managerial career had been just as undistinguished. In 1913, his first season as Boston's manager, the Braves finished fifth, 31 1/2 games behind the Giants. The prospects were not great.

Boston began 1914 in reverse and as late as July 19, Stallings' team was buried in last place. But then the Braves caught fire. Sparked by the second base-shortstop combination of Evers and Rabbit Maranville, the Braves began winning. Stallings was getting quality pitching from three unknowns—Dick Rudolph, Bill James and Lefty Tyler—and in early September, Boston moved into first place. The Braves wound up winning the pennant by 10 1/2 games over the Giants and then punctuated the accomplishment by sweeping Connie Mack's Philadelphia A's in the World Series. It was an ordinary team that for that one season accomplished the extraordinary and from that time on Boston's 1914 world champions were called "The Miracle Braves."

Joe Tinker, former shortstop for the Chicago Cubs, with some future baseball prospects.

Across town, the Braves' American League neighbors, the Red Sox, finished a solid second behind Philadelphia. They were 8 1/2 games back at the end of the season and when it became apparent they would not catch the A's, they decided to summon some young players from the minors. Among the recalls was a moon-faced 19-year-old pitcher who had a 22–9 record in the International League. There was no denying the promise of young George Herman Ruth, the kid they called Babe.

Ruth grew up tough in the streets of Baltimore where his father owned a saloon. He was largely ignored by his parents and wound up in an orphanage where he was introduced to the game of baseball. When Jack Dunn, owner of the Orioles, got wind of the barrel-chested boy with the perpetual grin, he went over to take a look. He was immediately impressed and agreed to adopt him and give him a job, employing him as a pitcher for his International League team. Ruth established his credentials in a hurry and Dunn sold his rights to the Red Sox who stashed him at Providence until season's end. Ruth arrived in Boston in time to win a couple of games but no one could have imagined at the time the ultimate impact he would have on the sport.

The Red Sox best pitcher when Ruth got to Boston was a left-hander named Dutch Leonard, who was in his second season. Leonard had been a sub-.500 pitcher as a rookie, going 14–16 although his 2.39 earned run average was impressive. Then, in 1914, Leonard bordered on the unhittable. He was 19–5 but set a record with a 1.01 ERA, the closest any pitcher with more than 200 innings of work has come to yielding less than a run a game.

Faced with financial pressures, Connie Mack broke up the Athletics following the 1914 season. Eddie Collins was sold to Chicago, Boston purchased Jack Barry and Herb Pennock, and pitcher Bob Shawkey went to New York. Eddie Plank and Chief Bender had headed for the Federal League and Home Run Baker retired. With its roster depleted, Philadelphia sank south in the standings, finishing in last place for seven straight years.

The Athletics' place at the top of the league was taken by Boston. The Red Sox had perhaps the best defensive outfield in history with Tris Speaker in center field flanked by Duffy Lewis in left and Harry Hooper in right. Ruth joined a pitching staff that included Rube Foster, Ernie Shore and Leonard. The Red Sox beat Detroit for the 1915 pennant and repeated by nipping Chicago in the 1916 race. And in those two seasons, Ruth began to emerge as the major figure of his time.

He was 18–8 with a 2.44 earned run average in his first full season and also batted .315 with four home runs in 92 at-bats.

A year later, he was ace of the Boston staff, going 23–12 and leading the league with nine shutouts and a 1.75 ERA. The Red Sox had passed up on him in the 1915 World Series, getting complete games in every start from Rube Foster, Ernie Shore and Dutch Leonard to beat the Phillies in five games. In 1916, however, they handed the ball to Babe in Game Two and he responded with a 14-inning complete game victory over Brooklyn, limiting the National League champions to six hits and winning 2–1. It remains the longest game in World

Tris Speaker played outfield for the Cleveland Indians and also served as the team's manager.

Series history.

The Red Sox finished second in 1917 with Ruth logging a 24–13 record and 2.02 ERA. He also was having quite an impact as a hitter, batting .325 and Boston manager Ed Barrow—the same man who would later be general manager of the New York Yankees—was beginning to get the idea that he might have more than a good pitcher on his hands with Ruth.

In 1917, the Babe was involved in one of the strangest games in baseball history. He was Boston's starting pitcher in the first game of a doubleheader at Washington. Ray Morgan was the leadoff hitter for the Senators and Ruth fell behind the batter. When umpire Brick Owens called ball four, Morgan trotted to first base while Ruth began arguing. As the discussion grew more heated—*The New York Times* said the umpire was struck behind the ear—Ruth had to be restrained by his teammates. He was ejected from the game and a hurry-up call to the Boston bullpen delivered Ernie Shore to relieve the angry Babe.

As Shore began pitching to Eddie Foster, Morgan tried to steal second. He was thrown out, and after he was retired, Shore set down the next 26 batters, completing a no-hitter. It is listed in the record books as a perfect game, the only one in which there was a runner on base and the only one in which the pitcher faced 26 hitters instead of 27.

A month before Shore's unusual no-hitter, the National League had a unique one of its own. In that game, Chicago's Hippo Vaughn faced Fred Toney of Cincinnati and for nine innings neither team was able to manage a hit. The double no-hit spell was broken in the 10th inning when Larry Kopf of the Reds singled and raced to third as Cy Williams dropped Hal Chase's fly ball. Jim Thorpe—yes, that Jim Thorpe—delivered the game's only run with another single.

Thorpe, the great Indian Olympian, spent almost his entire major league career with the New York Giants as a part-time player but had been sold to the Reds in April 1917. He was returned to New York in August, his stay in Cincinnati just long enough to be included in one of baseball's most unusual games.

Chase had spent his first eight years in the majors with the New York Highlanders, who later would become the Yankees. He managed the team for two seasons and was still the first baseman when Frank Chance, dismissed by the Cubs, arrived to manage the club in 1913. Chance knew enough about playing first base to suspect something was not quite right when balls kept eluding Chase. George Stallings, who also had managed the team before moving on to greater glory with the Miracle Braves of 1914, had also questioned Chase's dedication. Chance solved the problem by trading Chase to the White Sox and after a year in the Federal League, he surfaced in Cincinnati where he would win the batting championship in 1917. Still, the whispers persisted and in 1919, Chase was traded to McGraw's Giants. There he joined third baseman Heinie Zimmerman, who had become modern baseball's first Triple Crown winner in 1912 when he led the league in batting average, home runs and runs batted in, but had been a rather ordinary player after that. Both players were eyed somewhat warily by McGraw, who had serious questions about Zimmerman's .120

batting average during the 1917 World Series, and who had heard all the rumors about Chase. When league officials came up with a $500 canceled check paid to Chase by a known gambler, Zimmerman was confronted and confessed to a $250 bribe offer. McGraw was enraged and drove both players out of baseball.

The game, however, would soon be faced with a much larger, more serious scandal, one that threatened its very foundation. That happened in the 1919 World Series when the American League's Chicago franchise wrote the most sordid chapter in the game's history. That was the year the White Sox became known as the Black Sox.

Connie Mack, 1935.

THIRD INNING

3

RUIN AND RECOVERY 1919–1929

Charles Comiskey's largesse in paying the $10,000 bonus that Washington needed to keep Walter Johnson from fleeing to the Federal League was hardly characteristic for the owner of the Chicago White Sox. Comiskey had risen from the ranks, the only player ever to graduate to owner status. And he was not particularly interested in funding similar achievements for his employees.

Oh, it wasn't that Comiskey was a cheapskate. During World War I, he donated 10 percent of his gross receipts to the American Red Cross. But when it came to paying his players, Comiskey was considerably less generous.

Chicago had assembled a talented team that won the 1917 pennant and World Series. The stars were Eddie Collins, acquired from Philadelphia when Connie Mack began breaking up his "$100,000 infield," and Shoeless Joe Jackson, who came over from Cleveland where he had been the first rookie to hit .400. They were from opposite ends of the social scale, Collins equipped with a college education and Jackson nearly illiterate. Some

Joseph Jefferson ''Shoeless Joe'' Jackson in action during his heyday before the infamous ''Black Sox'' scandal.

where between those two extremes was Eddie Cicotte, a knuckleball pitcher who came over from Boston.

The White Sox were often an enigma, causing other players to wonder just what was going on with Comiskey's club. "You just never knew when they were going to go out there and beat your brains out or roll over and play dead," said Roger Peckinpaugh, then the shortstop for the New York Yankees. "Somebody was betting on those games, that's a cinch. When they wanted to play, you had a hard time beating them. That's how good they were."

Good enough, in fact, for Cicotte to win 29 games during the 1919 season. In the pennant race's final weeks, however, he disappeared from the pitching rotation. Suspecting something was up, especially since his contract promised a bonus for winning 30, Cicotte went to see Comiskey, looking for his extra money. The owner was not in a charitable mood.

"Why, Mr. Cicotte," he told the pitcher, "your contract calls for a bonus if you win 30 games. You have won 29. Twenty-nine wins is not 30 wins, Mr. Cicotte."

End of meeting.

Cicotte left suitably outraged, but that was a typical condition on this team. For the most part, Comiskey had managed to keep their salaries below the market level. Only Collins was making more than $10,000. The others were bargain basement players whose dislike for the boss was recharged every payday. This was a team ripe for the gamblers, a group that almost certainly would listen to proposals for improving their economic condition. And as America approached the Roaring '20s, there were plenty of gamblers around, only too willing to make the overtures.

The man who did it was Arnold Rothstein. Using ex-boxer Abe Atell as his bag man, Rothstein contacted a number of White Sox players with his proposal. The payoff would be $100,000, a sum that probably exceeded Comiskey's payroll for the entire team. The targets for the fix were Cicotte, the angry pitcher, Lefty Williams, the club's No. 2 pitcher, the slugging Jackson, first baseman Chick Gandil, third baseman Buck Weaver, center fielder Happy Felsch, shortstop Swede Risberg and reserve infielder Fred McMullin.

With five starters and the two best Chicago pitchers in on the plot, the Series began. Cicotte was on the mound for Chicago and the conspirators had arranged a signal that the deal was on. He would hit the leadoff batter with a pitch if the fix was in. Sure enough, Cicotte's second pitch plunked Morrie Rath in the back and the darkest chapter in baseball history began to take shape.

In the fourth inning of Game One, Cicotte gave up five straight hits and five runs as Cincinnati cruised to a 9–1 victory. In Game Two, control pitcher Lefty Williams walked six batters, four of them scoring. Behind the plate, White Sox catcher Ray Schalk couldn't figure out why both Cicotte and Williams had ignored his signals. Manager Kid Gleason wondered about the same thing.

In the press box, sportswriters well aware of rumors that the White Sox were doing business with gamblers,

Eddie Collins played with the Philadelphia Athletics before he was traded to Chicago.

scrutinized the performances. Ring Lardner, borrowing on a popular tune of the day, constructed this analysis to describe the Chicago club's performance:

"I'm forever blowing ball games,
"Pretty ball games in the air.
"I come from Chi
"Just go to bat and die.
"Fortune's coming my way,
"That's why I don't care.
"I'm forever blowing ball games
"And the gamblers treat us fair."

After Dickie Kerr pitched a shutout in Game Three, Cicotte came back for Game Four. In the fifth inning, he threw a tap back to the mound into the seats for a two-base error. Then, after a single to left, the pitcher deflected the throw to the plate, allowing the run to score as catcher Schalk howled. The pitcher's second error allowed the batter to reach second and he scored a moment later on another single. Final score: Cincinnati 2, Chicago 0.

Williams was beaten again in Game Five, giving up four runs in the sixth inning, a Reds' rally helped by an error by Happy Felsch. Cincinnati still needed one more victory to seal the Series, but Kerr came back to win Game Six 5–4 as Gandil drove in the winning run,

and Cicotte captured Game Seven 4–1. There has been speculation that the White Sox decided to play hard midway through the Series because they hadn't seen any money from the gamblers. Another theory is that the fixers wanted the White Sox to make it look more legitimate so as to avoid suspicion. And, as Roger Peckinpaugh had said, this team was good enough to win whenever it wanted to.

In Game Eight, Williams once again ignored Schalk's signals and tossed lollipop pitches to the Cincinnati hitters. He gave up four runs on four hits in the first inning and the Reds went on to a 10–5 victory to clinch the championship, one that most people seemed to agree was tainted. Comiskey, however, was having none of that fix talk, at least not right away. "I believe my boys fought the battles of the recent World Series on the level," he said. "And I would be the first to want information to the contrary. I would give $20,000 to anyone unearthing any information to that effect."

Ed Cicotte of the White Sox (before they became known as the "Black Sox" in a World Series scandal).

Eddie Collins, manager and second baseman of the Chicago White Sox and a Hall of Famer.

Commissioner Kenesaw Mountain Landis tossed out the first ball of the 1923 World Series at Yankee Stadium.

He never paid off on that bounty although eventually the case went to a grand jury that indicted the players and gamblers on a charge of conspiracy. The case lingered as baseball turned into a new decade and the owners, in an attempt to demonstrate that they could clean up their sport, established the office of the commissioner. The first man to hold the post was Kenesaw Mountain Landis, a federal judge who had been involved in the Federal League's antitrust challenge years before.

Landis was a no-nonsense commissioner and proved that early on in his administration. When a jury found the players and gamblers innocent of any criminal charges—it was during the trial that a Chicago youngster came up to Jackson on the steps of the courthouse and pleaded, "Say it ain't so, Joe"—Landis imposed his own penalties. He banned them from baseball, permanently.

The composite box score of the 1919 World Series reveals some interesting footnotes to the fix. Risberg batted .080 with four errors. Gandil hit .233 with one misplay. Williams lost all three of his starts and had a 6.61 earned run average. Cicotte was 1–2 with a 2.91 ERA. Felsch hit .231 with two errors. Weaver, who knew of the fix but allegedly had refused to participate, hit .324.

The strangest case of all may have been Jackson, who led all hitters with a .375 average, had 12 hits, four of them for extra bases, drove in six runs and made no errors.

Perhaps, as the boy on the courthouse steps had pleaded, in Shoeless Joe's case, it wasn't so.

Jackson had come to the majors with Philadelphia in 1908 but played just five games that season and five more the next year with the A's before being swapped to Cleveland. He batted .408 in 1911, his first full season, and starred with the Indians until 1915 when he

was swapped to the White Sox for three players and cash. He was one of baseball's very best hitters, finishing his career with a .356 average, third best in history. He wasn't a bad teacher, either. During the 1917 season, with Chicago on its way to the world championship, Shoeless Joe was approached by a Boston pitcher who was interested in copying Jackson's batting stance. The pitcher had displayed a pretty good stroke at the plate and there was talk of switching him from the mound to an everyday role to take advantage of his bat. So, Babe Ruth got some tips from Shoeless Joe Jackson.

Ruth hit .325 in 123 at-bats in 1917 and the next year, employing the help of Shoeless Joe, he slugged 11 home runs, tying Tilly Walker of Philadelphia for the league lead. He was 13–7 that year but it was becoming clear that Ruth's bat made him too much of an offensive force to be limited by his place in the pitching rotation. He had extended his World Series string of scoreless innings to 29 2/3 in 1918, a year in which he pitched in just 20 games but played in 72 others in the outfield and at first base.

By 1919, the Red Sox could not resist the temptation of having Ruth in the lineup, swinging his big bat every day.

He became a part-time pitcher, posting a 9–5 record and 2.97 ERA. And he turned into a fulltime slugger, smashing 29 home runs, far and away a major league record. The Babe was becoming something special but he would blossom not in Boston but in New York.

Red Sox owner Harry Frazee was in a bit of a financial squeeze, partly because of his penchant for backing Broadway plays that turned into busts. His prospect in the winter of 1919 was "No, No, Nanette" and he found willing wallets waiting for him in New York. The Yankees paid $125,000, a king's ransom in those days, for the oddly constructed Ruth, a huge man whose bulky body was supported by rail-thin legs. Yankee owners Jacob Ruppert and Colonel Tillinghast Huston also agreed to lend Frazee $300,000 and to hold the mortgage on Fenway Park. "No, No, Nanette" would go on—and so would the Babe.

In his first season in New York, Ruth merely launched 54 home runs and batted .376, driving in 137 runs. In most years, that would be good enough for the Triple Crown but, although he led in homers and RBIs, the Babe was fourth in batting average, trailing his tutor, Joe Jackson (.382), Tris Speaker (.388) and George Sisler (.407).

The home run, however, became his signature. He had a strange, almost mince-step trot around the bases that accentuated his unusual shape. He was a larger than life character, almost like a cartoon figure who had jumped off an artist's sketch pad and into a major league uniform. He had no concern about taking care of himself and chose instead to constantly feed his gargantuan appetite for all of life's excesses, nutritional and otherwise. Baseball historian Lee Allen once described Ruth's insatiable zest for adventure this way:

"He is a large man in a camel's hair coat and a camel's hair cap, standing in front of a hotel, his large nostrils sniffing the promise of the night."

Ruth was only one of a number of Boston players Harry Frazee sent to New York. The list included shortstop Everett Scott, catcher Wally Schang, pitchers Herb Pennock and Waite Hoyt, and, of course, the irrepressible Ruth. The first player to make the journey was an unpopular, brooding submarine pitcher named Carl Mays.

Mays quit the Red Sox in the middle of the 1919 season, accusing his teammates of not trying when he was pitching. The usual result of such a declaration of independence would be a suspension but Frazee chose instead to sell the pitcher's contract to the Yankees. Mays was 5–11 with the Red Sox that season but experienced an immediate turnaround in New York, going 9–3 for the Yankees.

Baseball commissioner Kenesaw Landis (center) with Babe Ruth (left) and Bob Meusel in 1922.

The Boston Red Sox outfield in 1919 featured (from left) Duffy Lewis, Tris Speaker and Harry Hooper.

Ty Cobb as Detroit manager, 1924.

Early in the 1920 season, before a frantic pennant race involving New York, Cleveland and Chicago began developing in the American League, the National League was the scene of one of baseball's strangest games, when the Brooklyn Dodgers and Boston Braves struggled 26 innings locked in a 1–1 tie—the longest game in major league history. The iron-armed pitchers who both went the distance that day were Joe Oeschger of the Braves and Leon Cadore of the Dodgers. For Oeschger, it was the second time he got stuck in a no-decision marathon against Brooklyn, having gone 20 innings in a similar stalemate the year before.

Ruth was having a monster first season with the Yankees and the club was locked in a tight race with Cleveland, managed by Tris Speaker, and Chicago, where rumors of the previous year's alleged World Series fix hung heavy over the White Sox.

In mid-August, the Indians came to New York for a crucial series with the Yankees. Cleveland had been swept by New York the week before at home and was looking for revenge. The Indians would face the submarine pitcher, Mays, in the first game of the Series and shortstop Ray Chapman, for one, was confident of his team's chances. "Tomorrow we ought to win pretty easily," he said on the eve of the Series. "I can't hit this man Mays, but the rest of the team sure can."

Cleveland led 3–0 as Chapman led off the top of the fifth inning. The first pitch from Mays was high and tight. Chapman, with bunt on his mind, was bent slightly forward and seemed anchored in the batter's box as the pitch smashed into his temple. The impact sent the ball rolling back to the mound and Mays played it as if it were a tap off Chapman's bat, throwing it to first baseman Wally Pipp. It was only then that the Yankees saw Chapman on the ground and realized what had happened. Twelve hours later, following brain surgery, Ray Chapman died, the only player ever killed in a major league game.

The Indians were devastated at the loss of their popular teammate. His replacement was a scared 21-year-old fresh off the campus of the University of Alabama. Joe Sewell was by no means convinced he could play major league ball at all, much less for a team locked in a pennant race. He was, of course, a better player than he was a scout and would enjoy a Hall of Fame career.

Cleveland's pennant chase was simplified late in the season when the Black Sox fixers were suspended. Chicago would finish two games behind, with New York three games back. And the Indians, wearing black armbands in Chapman's memory, went into the World Series against Brooklyn.

The opposing pitching staffs were anchored by spitball specialists, Burleigh Grimes for Brooklyn and Stan Coveleski for Cleveland. The Indians also had Jim Bagby, who led the league with 31 victories, while marathon man Leon Cadore and Rube Marquard backed Grimes for Brooklyn. The Indians would win the Series five games to two with Coveleski pitching three complete game victories and posting an ERA of 0.67. His feat was overshadowed, however, by Cleveland second baseman Bill Wambsganss, outfielder Elmer Smith and Bagby.

With the Series tied at 2–2, Game Five was set for Cleveland's Municipal Stadium. Grimes got in trouble immediately, yielding hits to the first three Indian batters. With the bases loaded, Smith came to the plate. In a year when Babe Ruth had hit 54 home runs, Elmer Smith had hit 12. But he jumped on one of Grimes' spitters and sent it over the right field fence for the first grand slam home run in World Series history.

When Bagby became the first pitcher to hit a Series homer, tagging a three-run shot in the fourth, Cleveland's lead was 7–0. So it was hardly cause for concern when Pete Kilduff and Otto Miller opened the top of the fifth for Brooklyn with singles. That brought up relief pitcher Clarence Mitchell, a decent enough hitter that he occasionally filled in at first base for the Dodgers.

Miller tagged a shot that seemed a certain base hit. Wambsganss raced to his right, leaped and speared the ball. His momentum brought him down just a few steps from second base. Kilduff had no chance to get back as Wambsganss stepped on the base. Now the fielder turned to see Otto Miller almost on top of him. He needed just a step or two to tag Miller, completing the only unassisted triple play in World Series history. The feat earned the Cleveland second baseman a permanent place in baseball history. It was a good thing, too, because his .154 batting average in that Series would not have done that.

If 54 home runs were not sufficient to thrust Ruth's Yankees to the top of the league, perhaps 59 would be. The Babe turned it up a notch in 1921, batting .378 and driving in 171 runs. Sure enough, New York finished in first place, beginning a stretch of six pennants in eight years for the team that would become baseball's most successful franchise. Fans were mesmerized by Ruth's prodigious power and it soon became clear to the proprietors of the Yankees that sharing the Polo Grounds, home of the National League Giants, was not tenable. So, on the other side of the Harlem River, construction began on Yankee Stadium, a handsome new structure that was called "The House that Ruth Built." Appropriately, the Babe homered on opening day there in 1923. That was the same year the Yankees wooed a 20-year-old first baseman off the campus of Columbia University, signing Lou Gehrig for a $1,500 bonus.

Gehrig was a part-timer until June 2, 1925, when Wally Pipp asked out of the lineup because of a headache. Manager Miller Huggins sent in the kid from Columbia and Gehrig stayed in for a record 2,130 consecutive games.

Lou Gehrig in training with the Yankees in 1924.

A year earlier, Washington called a temporary halt to a Yankee streak of three straight pennants, winning the American League flag for rookie manager Bucky Harris, who also played second base. The Senators did this while hitting just 22 home runs, 24 less than Ruth had by himself for second place New York. The Senators were led by Goose Goslin, who batted .344 and drove in a league-leading 129 runs, and Sam Rice, who hit .334 and led the league with 216 hits. The pitching staff still was constructed around the great Walter Johnson, who won 23 games and after 18 brilliant years would have his first chance to pitch in the showcase of the World Series.

The Senators were considered longshots against the New York Giants, who had won their fourth straight National League pennant. Twice, the Giants beat Johnson, but Washington hung tough and forced the Series to a decisive seventh game. New York was leading 3–1 in the bottom of the eighth inning when the Senators loaded the bases. Harris hit a sharp grounder to third that hopped over the shoulder of Fred Lindstrom, allowing the tying runs to score.

Now Johnson came out of the bullpen. Working on just one day's rest, he would have one last chance to win a World Series game and with it a world championship. For four innings, he shut the Giants out. Then, in the bottom of the 12th, Muddy Ruel lifted a high foul behind home plate. Catcher Hank Gowdy stumbled over his mask and was unable to make the play. Given a second chance, Ruel, who had only one previous hit in the Series, doubled. One batter later, Earl McNeely grounded toward Lindstrom at third. As the Giant infielder set himself for the play, the ball hit a pebble and bounced crazily over his head into left field, sending Ruel home with the winning run and giving Johnson his long-awaited World Series win, not to mention the Senators' longer-awaited world championship.

In 1926, it was another veteran pitcher's turn to shine in the spotlight of the World Series. This time it was Grover Cleveland Alexander, then 39 years old and acquired in mid-season by the St. Louis Cardinals from the Chicago Cubs. Alex seemed used up, a shadow of the pitcher who won 190 games in his first five major league seasons. But in this World Series, in the twilight of a brilliant career, Alexander reached back for one more sunrise.

After the Cardinals dropped the opener to New York, Alexander pitched a four-hitter in Game Two to even the Series. The Yankees lost Game Three but won the fourth and fifth to move within a single victory of the championship. But Alexander set them down in Game Six, 10–2, forcing the Series to a deciding seventh game. Alex went down to the bullpen with Jess Haines on the mound for St. Louis.

The Cardinals led 3–2 in the seventh inning but when New York loaded the bases with two out, St. Louis manager Rogers Hornsby went to the pen. The choice was Alexander to face rookie Tony Lazzeri. After a long foul ball, Alex, pitching with guts and guile, broke off a couple of classic curveballs to strike him out. He sailed through the eighth inning and got the first two batters in the ninth. That brought up Ruth, just the man the Yankees wanted in that circumstance, where one swing would tie the Series. But Alexander was having none

John McGraw, Ty Cobb and Rogers Hornsby, three baseball greats, meet during spring training in Sarasota, Florida, in 1927.

of that. He gave the Babe nothing to hit, walking him and then watching in wonder as the lumbering Ruth tried to steal second. When Bob O'Farrell's throw to Hornsby beat the Babe, the Cardinals were world champions and Alexander was a hero once more.

The Cardinals' accomplishment in winning that World Series was no small bit of business, for the Yankees had assembled a truly awesome lineup, one that would be known as Murderer's Row. Ruth was joined in the outfield by fleet Earle Combs in center and Bob Meusel in left. The third baseman was Joe Dugan, another bequest from Boston. Mark Koenig was at shortstop, Lazzeri handled second and Gehrig anchored the infield at first. Pat Collins was the catcher, handling a pitching staff constructed around Boston imports Waite Hoyt and Herb Pennock, Wilcey Moore and Urban Shocker. In 1927, those Yankees ravaged the American League, winning the pennant by 19 games.

Ruth hit 60 home runs, setting another single season record. Gehrig had 47. Ruth drove in 164 runs. Gehrig had 175. Together they formed perhaps the most fearsome 1–2 punch in baseball history. They batted .356 and .373 respectively and were surrounded with sluggers. Combs also hit .356. Meusel batted .307. The club batting average was a lusty .307.

Eddie Roush was traded from Cincinnati to the New York Giants to play center field in 1927.

Rogers Hornsby (center) signing contract with the Chicago Cubs in 1928. He is flanked by (left) William L. Veeck, president of the Cubs, and William Wrigley Jr., club owner.

This was an intimidating cast of characters, a lineup often cited as the most potent in baseball history. They swept four straight from Pittsburgh in the 1927 World Series and repeated the Series sweep a year later against St. Louis. And although New York slipped to second place behind Philadelphia in 1929, Babe Ruth's Yankees had stamped themselves as baseball's best team during the Golden Age of Sport. Boxing had Jack Dempsey. Tennis had Bill Tilden. Golf had Bobby Jones. Football had Red Grange.

But baseball had the Babe, the most legendary character of them all.

Walter Johnson, manager of the Washington Nationals, and Connie Mack, Philadelphia Athletics skipper, meet prior to the game on Opening Day of 1929.

Babe Ruth at bat in Fenway Park in Boston in 1929.

FOURTH INNING

SURVIVING THE DEPRESSION 1930–1939

Babe Ruth was a master of the moment. He was almost too good to be true, an invention perhaps of the imaginative writers of the day. Fifty years after he hit his last home run, a modern Yankee star named Don Mattingly confessed that he thought the Babe was a comic book character. He had to be. Surely, he couldn't be real. Not with some of his feats.

There were, for example, the Babe's medicinal qualities. Yankee lore is full of tales of Ruth visiting ailing youngsters in their hospital beds, promising them a home run and then going out and hitting one.

Or two.

Or even three.

Perhaps the best of those storybook tales occurred during the 1926 World Series, the one in which old Grover Alexander pitched the Cardinals to the world

championship with his courageous relief stint in the seventh game. Two days before Alex took over that Series, Ruth weaved a little medical magic.

On the eve of the Series, 11-year-old John Dale Sylvester fell ill in Essex Fells, New Jersey, with a serious case of blood poisoning. His father, a bank vice president, was desperate and in an attempt to buoy his son, he turned to the Yankees. Would Ruth hit one for the kid? Why, of course. Ruth, in fact, would hit three, setting a World Series record that lasted half a century. And John Dale Sylvester staged a miraculous recovery that doctors said began when the Babe started hitting homers.

Ruth was by no means a solitary star. Baseball was bursting with frontline performers during that period. It was the Babe's prodigious power, however, that

Babe Ruth on Opening Day 1932.

helped cleanse the sport of the dreary memory of the Black Sox scandal. He was the brightest star in a galaxy of great players.

Over in the National League, the wheelhouse was Rogers Hornsby, the slugging second baseman of the St. Louis Cardinals. Hornsby won six straight batting championships and seven in nine years. The string was highlighted by a .424 batting average in 1924—the highest single season production in major league history. There were other great offensive performers like the Waner brothers, Paul, who was called Big Poison, and Lloyd, known as Little Poison. Paul had 3,000 hits, three batting titles and hit over .300 14 times. Lloyd batted .355 as a rookie, setting a record with 223 hits and batted over .300 in 10 of his first 12 seasons.

There was Kiki Cuyler, who hit over .300 10 times and over .350 four times. There was George Sisler with a .340 career batting average and a record 257 hits in one season. There was Jimmie Foxx with 30 or more homers a record 12 straight seasons. And there was Al Simmons, who batted over .300 with more than 100 RBIs for 11 consecutive years.

In 1930, all the offensive components came together for an attack that sent pitchers running for cover. What kind of season was it? Well, the Philadelphia Phillies had a team batting average of .315. Chuck Klein batted .386, Lefty O'Doul hit .383 and Pinky Whitney batted .342. And with all that offense, the Phillies still finished in last place.

Bill Terry won the National League batting race with a .401 average and no NL hitter has cracked the .400 barrier since. For pure power, there was Hack Wilson of the Chicago Cubs, who walloped 56 home runs and drove in 190 runs. In all the years since Wilson conducted his assault on pitchers, no NL hitter has had more home runs in a season and no major league hitter has driven in more runs in a season.

Wilson batted .356 that year but it is a measure of the kind of offensive season it was that he didn't finish in the top 10 batting averages. He wasn't close to the top five in the National League, trailing Terry, Brooklyn's Billy Herman (.393), Klein, O'Doul and Fred Lindstrom of the New York Giants (.379). (Lindstrom hit .379 and finished fifth in the batting race.) Al Simmons won the American League batting title at .382, followed by Lou Gehrig (.379), Ruth (.359), Carl Reynolds of the Chicago White Sox (.359) and Mickey Cochrane of Philadelphia (.357). Imagine Wilson's consternation, hitting .356 and, thanks to Reynolds, not even having the best average in his own town.

There were 15 hitters with averages better than .340 and 17 who finished with more than 100 RBIs. But for the simple task of producing runs, nobody was close to Wilson, a fireplug of a man with a Ruthian-sized appetite for life's adventures. In 1930, he drove in 20 more runs and hit 16 more home runs than any other NL hitter.

The surge of offense echoed throughout baseball and, as the country struggled with the sad realities of an economic depression, the sport pressed on. When Ruth, at the height of his almost fictional accomplishments, signed an $80,000 contract (a deal comparable to about $300,000 in today's dollars), observers were astounded.

"Why, Babe," one newsman said to Ruth, "that's more than the President makes."

Ruth bit down on his trademark cigar, grinned widely and offered a perfectly logical explanation for the disparity.

"Well," he said, "I had a better year."

It was probably true. Ruth usually did. His numbers in 1930 were typical—49 home runs to lead the league and 153 RBIs, a neat accompaniment to Gehrig's 41 homers and 174 RBIs.

Babe Ruth scores a run and is congratulated by No. 4, teammate Lou Gehrig.

Rogers Hornsby played second base for St Louis.

Only two pitchers survived the offensive explosion with earned run averages of under 3.00. One was Brooklyn's Dazzy Vance, who was 17–15 with a 2.61 ERA for the fourth place Dodgers. The other was Lefty Grove of the Philadelphia A's, who seemed almost oblivious to the hitters, winning 28 games and posting a 2.54 ERA.

Five of Grove's wins that season came in relief and he saved nine other games for Connie Mack's A's. He was perfectly satisfied to pitch both ways for Philadelphia, which won the pennant by a comfortable margin. Grove had enjoyed a great season but it was just a prelude to 1931, when he bordered on the unbeatable.

From June 8 through August 19, Grove won 16 consecutive games, matching the AL record set in 1912 by Smoky Joe Wood and Walter Johnson. The streak finally ended on August 22, when Dick Coffman of the St. Louis Browns handcuffed Philadelphia on three hits, beating Grove 1–0. It was one of just four games he lost all year—the others by scores of 2–1, 7–5 and 4–3. Grove's 31 victories stood as the league record until 1968 when Denny McLain of the Detroit Tigers matched it.

Grove was a control artist and led the league in strikeouts for the seventh straight season in 1931. His 2.06 ERA was 57 points lower than runnerup Lefty Gomez of the New York Yankees. Even with all the slugging going on around him, Grove was an easy winner of the first official Most Valuable Player award in the American League. And that in a year when Al Simmons won his second straight batting title, hitting .390, and Lou Gehrig hit 46 homes and drove in 184 runs.

In the National League, St. Louis was assembling the team that would be known as the Gashouse Gang, a cast of characters who played the games as if their very lives depended on the outcome. They had lost to the A's in the 1930 World Series, limited to 12 runs in six games by Grove and George Earnshaw, who did the bulk of Philadelphia's pitching. And when the 1931 Series turned into a rematch, St. Louis vowed it would get revenge.

The symbol of those chip-on-the-shoulder Cardinals was Johnny Leonard Roosevelt Martin, a plucky 5-foot-8 outfielder whose pals called him Pepper. Martin, in his first full major league season, had batted .300, nothing special on the Cardinals, whose attack was constructed around Chick Hafey, who led the league with a .349 average, Jim Bottomly, who finished a single point behind at .348, and Frankie Frisch, who hit .311.

Martin was a head-first slide guy, givng no quarter and asking none. His fierce determination made him a crowd favorite and his nickname—the Wild Horse of the Osage—was as much a tribute to his style as it was to his production. But in the 1931 World Series, nobody produced better than he did.

Both the A's and Cards won their pennants comfortably, St. Louis coasting home 13 games in front of John McGraw's last Giant team, and Philadelphia holding off the offensive assault of the Ruth-Gehrig Yankees by 13½ games. For the Series opener, Connie Mack handed the baseball to Grove and his 31-game winner won, 6–2. The only interference came from the brash rookie, Martin, who had two singles, a double and a stolen base. In Game Two, however, Martin really took over.

In the second inning, he stretched a single into a double with a head-first slide. Then he stole third and scored on a sacrifice fly. In the seventh, he singled, stole second, advanced to third on an infield out and scored on a squeeze bunt as the Cards won 2–0 behind Bill Hallahan.

With Grove back on the mound for Philadelphia in Game Three, Martin had two more hits and scored twice in a 5–2 St. Louis victory. He had both Cardinal hits as Earnshaw shut St. Louis out 3–0 in Game Four. He also stole another base as he continued to harass the A's at every turn.

Game Five turned into a virtuoso performance for Martin. He beat out a bunt in the fourth inning, homered in the sixth, and singled in the eighth. He finished the day with four runs batted in as St. Louis won, 5–1.

At that point, Martin had 12 hits in 18 at-bats and

Umpire signals ''safe' as the Yankees' Babe Ruth slides into second base during a 1931 game against the Boston Red Sox.

even though he went hitless in Games Six and Seven, he still finished the Series batting .500 with five stolen bases. The 12 hits were a record and even though he was shut out at bat in the last two games, the Cardinals' triumph belonged to him, especially when he came tearing in to grab Max Bishop's low line drive for the final out in Game Seven.

Martin was a pesky player, never a long ball threat, and he epitomized the Gashouse Gang's approach to baseball. Home runs were not a major part of their arsenal. That, of course, was not the case with the Gehrig-Ruth Yankees, who became known as the Bronx Bombers because of their ability to hit the ball into the seats.

They complemented each other beautifully in the middle of the Yankee lineup, Ruth batting third and Gehrig fourth. Each had 13 years with more than 100 RBIs. Seven times, Gehrig's RBI total soared past 150 and his 184 in 1930 were just six short of Hack Wilson's major league record. And although Ruth, with his magic total of 714 homers, was considered the Yankees' Sultan of Swat, Gehrig had some pop in his bat as well, totaling 493 homers.

Three Philadelphia Athletics, (from left) catcher Mickey Cochrane, manager Connie Mack and pitcher Robert "Lefty" Grove, prepare to meet the St. Louis Cardinals.

In the summer of 1932, Jimmie Foxx made a run at Ruth's record of 60 home runs, set five years earlier. The muscular Philadelphia first baseman finished with 58. That was 24 more than Gehrig and 17 more than Ruth but it was the two Yankee sluggers who had the most memorable homers of that season.

On June 4, the Yankees were in Philadelphia, winning a rather shabby game, 20–13. The contest might otherwise have been forgettable except for Gehrig, who hit four consecutive home runs, the first man to accomplish that feat in modern baseball history. He drove in six runs and came within a few feet of a fifth home run when Al Simmons ran down his long drive in the ninth.

But like so many of Gehrig's accomplishments that were overshadowed by Ruth, the four home runs were nearly overlooked because the big news in New York baseball that day was the abrupt resignation of John McGraw as manager of the Giants. McGraw had ruled

Babe Ruth connects off the Athletics' Lefty Grove in a game at Yankee Stadium early in the 1932 season.

the team with an iron hand for 31 years, winning 10 pennants. Now, at age 59, the old Oriole turned over the team to Bill Terry, moving on to the front office. His choice of Terry to succeed him was somewhat ironic because the two had feuded and McGraw had not talked to his star first baseman for years.

Murderer's Row was in full flower at Yankee Stadium. New York's lineup was almost frightening. Ruth (.341, 41 home runs, 137 RBIs) and Gehrig (.349, 34 homers, 151 RBIs) had typical seasons. Surrounding them were Tony Lazzeri (.300, 113 RBIs), Ben Chapman (.299, 107 RBIs) and Bill Dickey (.310, 84 RBIs). New York won the pennant by 13 games and arrived at the World Series eager to flex its muscles against the Chicago Cubs, who had finished four games in front in the National League, following a mid-season managerial switch from Rogers Hornsby to first baseman Charlie Grimm.

The Cubs had no match for Yankee power. They hit just 69 home runs compared to 160 for New York. But there were four .300 hitters in the Chicago lineup—Grimm (.307), Billy Herman (.314), Riggs Stephenson (.324) and Johnny Moore (.305). Two other starters, Kiki Cuyler and Gabby Hartnett, were headed for the Hall of Fame.

There were bad feelings between the teams before the first pitch. New York manager Joe McCarthy had spent five seasons as the Cubs' pilot, winning the pennant in 1929. But the situation turned sour for him and he left the club in the final week of the 1930 season, undermined, he felt, by Hornsby, who took his job. Horns-

Lou Gehrig, 1935.

Babe Ruth (left) and Lou Gehrig head for Yankee dugout after Gehrig homered in the first game of the World Series in 1932.

by was gone by the 1932 Series, but the bitterness McCarthy felt for the Cubs persisted. And it spread to his team, largely because of an old teammate.

Shortstop Mark Koenig had spent four full seasons in New York before being dispatched to Detroit in 1930 in a five-player exchange that seemed to have little significance at the time. Certainly Ownie Carroll, Yats Wuestling and Harry Rice—the players New York acquired in the trade—made no great impact on Yankee fortunes. Koenig batted .240 in 76 games for the Tigers and then became backup to Billy Rogell the next year, batting .253 in 106 games. By 1932, he had drifted to the minors but his career took an abrupt turn when,

in late August, the Cubs brought him back to the majors. In the season's last 33 games, Koenig batted a lusty .353 and helped Chicago nail down the pennant. For his contribution, the Cubs voted Koenig a half-share of their World Series booty, a bit of penurious behavior that outraged the shortstop's old friends in New York.

The Yankees decided there was a simple explanation for the Cubs' less-than-generous treatment of their old pal, Koenig. Chicago's players were plainly cheapskates and the Yankees weren't shy about saying so. The Cubs were outraged that the Yankees, those high and mighty bigshots from New York, were sticking their noses in an an affair that was none of their business.

So, feelings were running high and the bench-jockeying was in high gear as the two teams met in the Series. The name-calling got pretty severe, especially after the Yankees won the first two games in New York and then traveled to Chicago where the fans got into it.

The main target, as usual, was Ruth—highly visible, the man always in the middle of almost everything that took place on the field. He was a pretty good bench jockey in his own right, perfectly capable of giving back every bit as much as he got. So, when he came to bat in the fifth inning of Game Three, Wrigley Field was in something of an uproar, much of the din originating from the Cubs' dugout.

Charlie Root was on the mound for Chicago. His first pitch was called a strike. Then, after two balls, Root threw another strike. Now, with the place howling, Ruth made a gesture. The question was just what he had in mind. Some interpreted the signal to the Cubs and Root that he still had one strike left. Others thought he was pointing to the center field stands, indicating where he planned to hit the next pitch. Another version was that he was responding to some particularly nasty needling from Cub pitcher Guy Bush, pointing to the pitcher's mound, where Bush would be spending the next day.

Whatever it was that Ruth meant, the result was one of the most memorable home runs in World Series history, a towering blow that became known as Ruth's Called Shot. Was that really what it was, an arrogant prediction of a homer on a two-strike pitch that left little margin for error? Or was it mere happenstance, a fortunate turn of circumstances for a man who had a knack for turning circumstances fortunate?

Ruth had tagged Root for a three-run homer in the first inning, so it is entirely likely that the Cub pitcher, hardly the Milquetoast type, would have had the Babe rolling in the dirt from a high hard one if he thought Ruth was trying to show him up by predicting another one. Nevertheless, that was how many people saw it.

For his part, Ruth was reticent at first about claiming that he had indeed called his home run. But as the years went by and the tale was embellished, he did little to suggest that he had not done exactly that.

Called or not, the home run was the last one Ruth would hit in World Series play. Lost in the excitement of that homer were two by Gehrig, who batted .529 with three home runs, nine runs scored and eight driven in as the Yankees completed a four-game sweep. If there had been a World Series MVP in those days, it would have been the strapping first baseman, even though the Series is best remembered for Ruth's shot—called or not.

Joe Cronin, with the Washington Senators in 1933.

Pittsburgh infielder Pie Traynor at training camp in 1932.

Because of economic conditions in the country, baseball attendance was soft and the game was anxious to promote itself in any way it could. It took the sports editor of the *Chicago Tribune* to come up with a vehicle. Since the World's Fair was in Chicago, Arch Ward reasoned that it would be a smart idea to gather the best baseball players of the time and let them play against each other for charity. The All-Star Game would be a one-shot affair that baseball viewed as a shot-in-the-arm promotion. It turned into much more than that.

The game would be played in Comiskey Park with John McGraw lured out of retirement to manage the National League and Connie Mack piloting the American League stars. Fans were asked to vote for their favorite players and it was no great surprise that Babe Ruth led the balloting with 10,000 votes. Even at age 38, and approaching the end of a fabulous career, Ruth remained the game's No. 1 attraction.

By the time the All-Stars were assembled, Ruth was approaching the 700th home run of his career, no small accomplishment since that was more than twice as many as any other player had accumulated. So it was a given that he would start in his accustomed spot of right field for the AL. With Al Simmons in center field, Lou Gehrig at first, Charley Gehringer at second, Joe Cronin at short, Rick Ferrell catching and Lefty Gomez pitching, Mack had seven future Hall of Famers in his starting lineup.

The National League stars were no less impressive. McGraw had his successor, Bill Terry, at first base, Frankie Frisch at second, and Chuck Klein in the outfield with Paul Waner, Pie Traynor and Gabby Hartnett coming off the bench.

Gabby Hartnett in 1930.

Giant manager and first baseman Bill Terry.

But in that setting, it is impossible to think of anyone other than Ruth standing center stage. And the Babe did not disappoint the 49,000 fans who jammed Comiskey for this show.

The AL stars scored first, nicking Wild Bill Hallahan for a run in the second. With one out, Jimmy Dykes and Joe Cronin walked. After Rick Ferrell flied out, Lefty Gomez came to the plate. Gomez was the best excuse baseball ever had to invent the contrived offensive weapon of a designated hitter. Lefty could pitch, but he simply couldn't hit. He was an automatic out most of the time. But this time, Gomez stroked a single and assured himself a place in baseball histroy as the unlikely owner of the first RBI in All-Star Game history. Years later, he loved reliving the moment, telling and retelling the story of his hit, proof positive, he said, that he wasn't as bad a hitter as everyone said.

An inning later, Hallahan walked Gehringer for the second time. In the first inning, Gehringer had walked and stolen second, putting a man in scoring position for Ruth. Hallahan had struck Ruth out that time. He would not be so fortunate two innings later.

He started Ruth inside, missing with his first pitch and then catching the outside corner for a strike. Then, on the 1–1 pitch, Ruth swung and sent a low line drive that curled around the right field foul pole for a dramatic home run.

Later, Ruth went to the wall to take a potential home run away from Chick Hafey and help preserve the 4–2 American League victory. The game presented stark contrasts in the styles of the two managers. McGraw viewed it as an exhibition and substituted freely, much in the fashion that modern managers operate with All-Star teams. Mack, on the other hand, went about it as business as usual, substituting sparingly and leaving established stars like Jimmie Foxx, Bill Dickey and Tony Lazzeri sitting on the bench.

Vernon ''Lefty'' Gomez.

Babe Ruth crossing home plate after a two-run home run off National League starting pitcher Bill Hallahan in the first All Star Game, 1933. Greeting Babe Ruth is teammate Lou Gehrig (left).

President Roosevelt throwing out the first ball to start the third game of the World Series. Holding his other arm is Joe Cronin of the Washington Senators.

For Foxx, it was one of the few disappointments in an otherwise brilliant season. Coming off his 58 home run year, the Philadelphia slugger won the Triple Crown, leading the American League in hitting (.356), home runs (48) and runs batted in (163). But just as Hack Wilson had to share Chicago's spotlight in his big 56 home run, 190-RBI season, Foxx had Triple Crown company in his own town in 1933. The Phillies' Chuck Klein led the National League in hitting (.356), home runs (28) and RBIs (120).

The Triple Crown is a rarely accomplished feat, but Foxx came remarkably close to doing it two years in a row. In his 58-homer season, the man they called Double X led the league with 169 RBIs and batted .364, just three points short of Dale Alexander's .367. Foxx actually hit 60 home runs that season, matching Ruth's record, but two of his homers were rained out, coming in games that were called by weather before they were complete.

Klein's Triple Crown came a year after he was named National League MVP and there was a bit of irony attached to it. Each of his numbers when he led the league in batting, home runs and RBIs in 1933 was short of his 1930 production of .386, 40 homers and 170 RBIs, when he failed to lead the league in any of those offensive categories. He did throw out 44 runners that season, setting an assists record that still stands.

McGraw's last pitcher in that first All-Star Game was a left-handed screwball specialist from the New York Giants. Carl Hubbell pitched two scoreless innings that day, but that was really nothing new for him. Four days before the All-Star Game, Hubbell went to the mound for the Giants against St. Louis and beat the Cards 1–0 in a game that stretched over 18 innings. He allowed just six hits, never more than one in an inning, and struck out 12 St. Louis hitters without allowing a base on balls.

A week after the All-Star Game, Hubbell started stringing goose-eggs again. From July 13 through August 1, the screwball expert did not allow a run for 46 consecutive innings, a record that lasted 35 years until Don Drysdale cracked it in 1968.

Hubbell would win 23 games and lead the league with a 1.66 earned run average that season as the cornerstone of the Giants' rush to the National League pennant. New York defeated Washington in five games for its first world championship since 1922. A few months later, with his team on top once more, John McGraw died at the age of 60.

Jimmie Foxx at spring training in 1938.

Carl Hubbell, 1932.

Hubbell would win 253 games in his career but is best remembered for a remarkable feat in the 1934 All-Star Game. The success of the first All-Star gathering persuaded baseball that it had stumbled on to something and so the game's best players were reunited a year later in New York. Lefty Gomez, owner of the first All-Star RBI and on his way to a 26–5 season for the Yankees, started for the AL and Hubbell was on the mound for the Nationals.

Charlie Gehringer led off the game with a single and reached second when Wally Berger bobbled the ball. When Heinie Manush walked, the AL was in business with the meat of it batting order coming up.

First was Ruth. Hubbell got him in a 1–2 hole and then slipped the screwball past him for strike three.

Next was Lou Gehrig, who swung and missed at a third strike as Gehringer and Manush pulled a double steal.

Now it was Jimmie Foxx' turn. He went down on three pitches.

Al Simmons was the first American League batter in the second inning and Hubbell's screwball was still working its magic. He was gone on four pitches, another strikeout victim. Four pitches later, Joe Cronin had gone down on strikes, as well.

Five Hall of Fame sluggers. Five straight strikeouts. It was a brilliant bit of pitching, a moment recalled annually at All-Star Games. The irony of Hubbell's performance is that it came in a game that turned into a slugfest with the American League prevailing, 9–7.

Opposite, at top: Carl Hubbell (left) of the Giants and Vernon "Lefty" Gomez of the Yankees, starting pitchers in the 1934 All Star Game.

Carl Hubbell in spring training, 1937.

American League sluggers (left to right) Al Simmons, Lou Gehrig, Babe Ruth, and Jimmie Foxx before the 1934 All Star Game.

Dizzy Dean.

Before the start of the 1934 season, the Giants were in position to lord it over the rest of New York. They owned the town. Ruth's star was clearly in decline. He was 39 now and although he still had home run power, his totals were going down. The Giants, not the Yankees, were the reigning world champions.

In spring training, Bill Terry was discussing his team's prospects as well as the rest of the National League when somebody asked about Brooklyn. The Dodgers were a rather comical cast of characters who had managed to finish above fourth place only twice in the 13 years since they had last won a pennant. They were part of the New York equation only because of geography. To mention the Dodgers in the same breath as the Giants and Yankees, well, that bordered on heresy. Ter-

Bill Terry at bat.

ry considered the question and then offered one of baseball's most famous replies, one he would later regret.

"Brooklyn?" he sneered. "Is Brooklyn still in the league?"

It was a slap in the face that would come back to haunt the Giants before season's end. For much of the summer, Terry's talented team was leading the race. Then the Cardinals' Gashouse Gang got hot. Sparked by a big, old country boy pitcher named Jay Dean—you can call him Dizzy—St. Louis ran off a 33–12 stretch and with two days left in the season, the teams were tied. Both clubs would finish at home, the Cardinals against the last place Cincinnati Reds, the Giants against—well, well, what a coincidence—the Brooklyn Dodgers, who were, of course, still in the league.

Babe Ruth with Jimmie Foxx before the season opener in 1934.

Casey Stengel (left) is probably best known as manager of the Yankees and Mets, but he also managed the Brooklyn Dodgers. He is seen here with Brooklyn catcher Al Lopez at Ebbets Field in 1934. Both are in the Hall of Fame.

Casey Stengel's Dodgers came into the final series on a mission. This was a chance to feed some crow to their high-faluting crosstown rivals who rarely took Brooklyn seriously. The Dodgers were serious this time, beating the Giants 5–1 behind Van Lingle Mungo while the Cardinals were clinching a tie for the pennant with a victory over Cincinnati. Then Brooklyn sealed New York's fate, wiping out a four-run deficit to defeat the Giants 8–5, and making the Cardinals the pennant winners.

The Gashouse Gang was managed by its second baseman, Frankie Frisch, who hit .305. The bulk of the offense, however, came from first baseman Rip Collins, who hit .333 with a league-leading 35 home runs and 128 RBIs, and outfielder Joe Medwick (.319, 18 home runs, 106 RBIs).

In the American League, Connie Mack's pocket was being pinched by the Depression and the owner of the A's solved that problem as he had once before, by selling off his best players for much-needed cash. Slugger Al Simmons, third baseman Jimmy Dykes and pitcher George Earnshaw went to Chicago. First baseman Jimmie Foxx and pitcher Lefty Grove were shipped to Boston, and catcher Mickey Cochrane was dispatched to Detroit, where he would double as manager of the Tigers.

Johnny Mize, ''the $55,000 rookie,'' in 1935. The Cincinnati Reds turned him back to the St. Louis Cardinals after they learned he needed a leg operation.

Johnny Mize gets his greeting from teammates on the St. Louis Gashouse Gang after hitting a home run against Chicago in 1936.

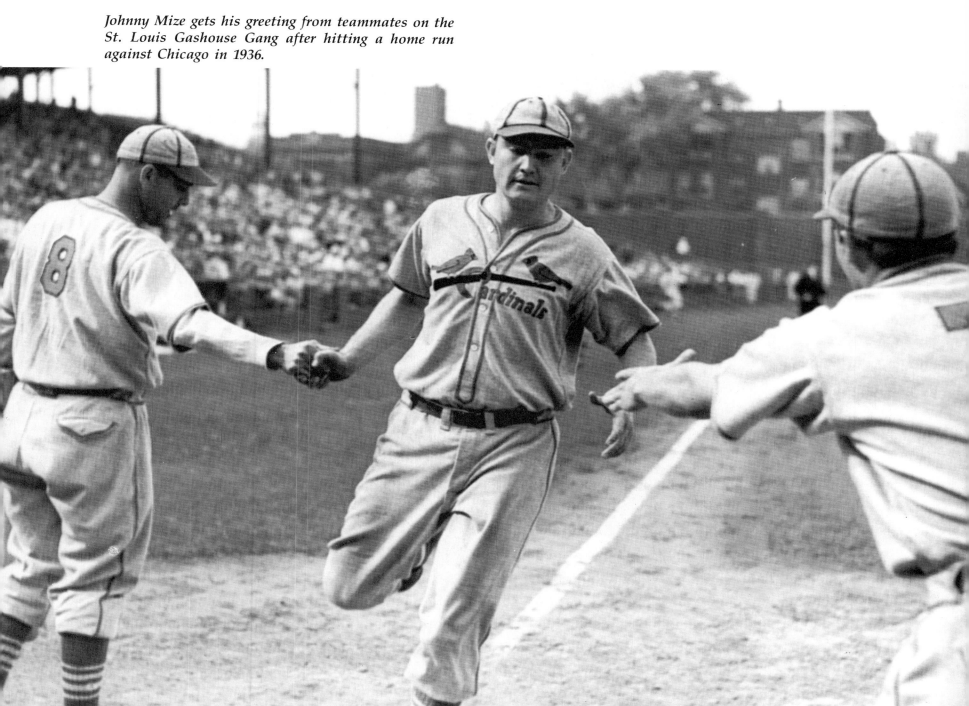

Detroit had not won a pennant since the Ty Cobb days of 1909 but that all changed under Cochrane, who took the Tigers to the top. He had plenty of help doing it. Six of Detroit's eight regulars hit better than .300, led by Charlie Gehringer, who batted .356 and drove in 127 runs. Four Tigers drove in more than 100 runs, including a slugging young first baseman named Hank Greenberg, who hit .339. On the mound, Detroit had Schoolboy Rowe, who won 24 games including a record-tying 16 in a row, and Tommy Bridges, a 22-game winner.

With productive seasons from Marv Owen (.317, 96 RBIs), Goose Goslin (.305, 100 RBIs) and JoJo White (.313), Cochrane brought the Tigers home four games ahead of New York, where age was catching up with Babe Ruth. Lou Gehrig won the Triple Crown, leading the league in batting average (.363), home runs (49), and RBIs (165), and even though the Yankees finished second, it wasn't exactly a washout year for New York. That's because in mid-season, they invested $25,000 to purchase a minor league outfielder from the San Francisco Seals. Other clubs had been scared off by the kid's knee injury but the Yankees thought Joe DiMaggio was worth the gamble.

Mickey Cochrane of the Detroit Tigers in his second season as manager-catcher in 1935. Detroit won the American League pennant the previous year.

Mickey Cochrane crossing the plate with the winning run in Detroit's World Series win over the Cubs in 1935. It was Detroit's first baseball title.

Detroit catcher-manager Mickey Cochrane prepares to apply the tag to Cubs shortstop Billy Jurges in the 1935 World Series.

The World Series was an intriguing matchup between the Gashouse Gang of the Cardinals and the long-absent Tigers. Dizzy Dean dealing with Charlie Gehringer and Hank Greenberg, Schoolboy Rowe up against Joe Medwick and Rip Collins.

Dean was a folk hero in St. Louis. Energized by the presence of his brother, Paul, on the Cardinal pitching staff, Dean had predicted a banner season. "Me and Paul will win 50 games," he predicted during spring training. It sounded like arrogant boasting, but the fact of the matter is they came tantalizingly close to the goal when Dizzy won 30 and his brother—affectionately called Daffy—added 19. And then Dizzy explained, "If you do something, it ain't boastin'."

Dizzy won the Series opener and Daffy took Game Three. In Game Four, Dizzy was sent in as a pinch run-

Dizzy Dean in 1935.

Hank Greenberg at practice in 1935.

ner and neglected to slide going into second. Tiger shortstop Billy Rogell's throw to first caught the Cardinal ace flush on the forehead, sending him to the hospital. Headlines the next day, written perhaps with tongue in cheek, said: "X-rays of Dean's Head Show Nothing." Dizzy was back on the mound for Game Five but the Tigers beat him 3–1 to move within one game of the world championship.

With the Series back in Detroit, Paul Dean took Game Six, driving in the winning run himself with a single. For Game Seven, Dizzy was back for his third start and St. Louis made it easy for him, scoring seven runs in the third inning. By the sixth, the score was 9–0 when Medwick went barreling into third base on a triple— his 11th hit of the Series. Marv Owen faked a tag and the two players tangled briefly with no particular

damage. But when Medwick took his position in left field, he was greeted by a shower of refuse thrown by angry Tiger fans. They threw bottles, fruit, anything they could find. At first, Medwick tossed pieces of debris to Pepper Martin in a game of catch. Soon, though, he was forced to retreat from the barrage. Three times he left the field and each time he returned, the situation turned uglier, finally bordering on a riot.

In his field box, commissioner Kenesaw Mountain Landis surveyed the scene. Finally he called Medwick and St. Louis manager Frankie Frisch over and decided to order the outfielder out of the game for his own protection. With the score 11–0, it hardly effected the outcome but it does remain as one of the darker moments in World Series history.

Lefty Grove (left) and Dizzy Dean before the 1936 All Star Game.

In the winter of 1934, the marriage of Babe Ruth and the Yankees finally ended. Age had taken its toll on the Babe and the Yankees had no intention of obliging his often-stated wish to manage the team. So they simply released him. It freed the Babe to return to Boston, this time with the National League Braves, to be used primarily as a gate attraction. His once potent bat was merely a memory now and as the 1935 season turned into June, he decided to retire. But before he left, there was one last performance at center stage. On May 25 in Pittsburgh, Ruth was the young slugger once more, launching three home runs—Nos. 712, 713 and 714 of his fabulous career. A week later, on June 2, he was done.

Babe Ruth hits a run-scoring single in his first National League at-bat with the Boston Braves in 1935. He homered later in the game.

Babe Ruth, after the last game of his career as a Yankee, September 30, 1934.

Meanwhile, his replacement was having one last big season in the Pacific Coast League before heading for New York. Joe DiMaggio batted.398 that year with 270 hits. His knee was sound and suddenly, the Yankees' $25,000 gamble was looking awfully good.

DiMaggio was just 21 years old when he got to New York but he batted .323 with 29 home runs and 125 RBIs in his rookie season. There was no pressure on the kid because Lou Gehrig was enjoying an MVP season, hitting .354 with 49 homers and 152 RBIs and Bill Dickey was batting .362, the highest average ever for a catcher.

It was the start of another Yankee dynasty—the first of four straight world championship seasons. They shrugged off the New York Giants in the 1936 World Series, even beating Carl Hubbell, who had finished the season with 16 consecutive victories and would tack eight more wins on to the streak in 1937. Hubbell was

Lou Gehrig (left) and Joe DiMaggio in front of Yankee dugout in 1936.

26–6 with a 2.31 earned run average that season but when the Yankees whipped him 5–2 in Game Four it put them in control of the Series that they would win in six games.

The Giants were back to try the Yankees again in 1937 and again the Yankees prevailed, this time in just five games. Manager Joe McCarthy's team just had too many answers with stars like Gehrig (.351, 37 home runs, 159 RBIs), DiMaggio (.346, 46 home runs, 167, RBIs) and Dickey (.332, 29 home runs, 133 RBIs) punishing opposing pitchers.

Typical of the Yankee attack was second baseman Tony Lazzeri, a solid performer who hit .292 in his career but never would be mistaken for one of the power guys like Gehrig, Ruth or DiMaggio. On May 24, 1936, however, Lazzeri did something those sluggers never managed. In a game at Philadelphia, the Yankee second baseman drilled three home runs, two of them with the bases loaded. He came within inches of a fourth homer, settling instead for a two-run triple and

11 runs batted in for the day. Nobody, not Gehrig, not DiMaggio, not Ruth, ever drove in more in an American League game.

When Ruth retired, he left behind a plethora of home run records, the most famous his 60 in a season and 714 in a career. In 1927, the year he hit 60, 17 of his homers came in September, another record. Two years after he hit his last homer, the first of Ruth's records fell under an assault by Detroit's Rudy York, who walloped 18 homers during the month of August 1937. A year later, York's teammate, Hank Greenberg, made a heroic run at Ruth's single season record, finishing with 58. He was shut out in the final five games of the season, his bid buried in a barrage of bases on balls. Greenberg was less than devastated by his failure to break the record.

"I never compared myself to the Babe," he said in his autobiography. "I wasn't that kind of home run hitter. My goal in baseball was always RBIs, to break Gehrig's record of 184 RBIs. I would have loved to do that."

In fact, noboby came closer. Greenberg drove in 183 runs in 1937 but couldn't prevent the Tigers from finishing a fat 13 games behind New York.

New York Giants' pitcher Carl Hubbell receiving the Most Valuable Player Award for 1936 from James Dawson (left), president of the Baseball Writer's Association, with Ford Frick, National League president, looking on.

Manager Bill Terry watching his Giants at batting practice before the 1937 World Series.

Giant and Yankee greats Bill Terry (left) and Joe McCarthy, before the World Series opener in 1937.

Opposite, top: Mel Ott, with characteristic raised leg batting stance, at bat for the Giants in 1936.

Opposite, bottom: Yankee pitcher Vernon Gomez (left), manager Joe McCarthy, and catcher Bill Dickey before the 1937 World Series opener.

Vander Meer warming up.

In the first night game in the East, Johnny Vander Meer pitched a no-hitter for the Cincinnati Reds against the Brooklyn Dodgers, June 15, 1938—his second no-hitter in a week.

As baseball struggled with the economic realities of the Depression, it sought ways to get fans out to the ballpark. One solution was to play the games when the fans were available—at night. Cincinnati was the first team to try it and attracted 25,000 to a game in May 1935. Three years later, New York gots its first night game and left-hander Johnny Vander Meer of the Reds made sure it would never be forgotten.

Vander Meer, a high-kicking 22-year-old, had pitched a no-hitter against Boston on June 11 and his next start would be in Brooklyn on June 15, where the Dodgers would introduce night baseball to the New York metropolitan area. For eight innings, he baffled Brook-lyn and when he got Buddy Hassett leading off the ninth, he was just two outs away. Suddenly, however, his control abandoned him and Vander Meer walked Babe Phelps, Cookie Lavagetto and Dolph Camilli, load-ing the bases. "I was trying too hard, pressing myself," he would say years later.

Vander Meer took a deep breath and went back to work. Ernie Koy tapped into a force play at the plate and then Leo Durocher sent a lazy fly ball to Harry Craft, completing a second straight no-hitter for the Reds' southpaw. It remains a feat unmatched in base-ball history.

Despite Vander Meer's remarkable achievement, the Reds could finish no better than fourth. The pennant race in the NL came down to Chicago and Pittsburgh and a late September series in Wrigley Field. The Pirates came into town with a game-and-a-half lead but the Cubs won the opener, 2–1, behind Dizzy Dean, who had come over from the Cardinals. That shaved the lead to a half-game and first place was on the line the next day when the teams battled through eight innings tied at 5–5.

With darkness setting in, it seemed almost certain that this game would end in a tie and be replayed the next day. But then Gabby Hartnett, the player-manager of the Cubs, hit a home run in the bottom of the ninth for the victory. Because of the overcast conditions, Hartnett's homer became known as "the homer in the gloamin'." The Pirates never recovered. They lost again the next day and the Cubs went on to win the pennant, only to be steamrolled by the Yankees in four straight games in the World Series.

That Series sweep was accomplished with precious little contribution from Lou Gehrig, a tower of Yankee strength for years. He was limited to four singles but his problems were overlooked as Yankee pitching limited Chicago to nine runs in the four games.

Gehrig was still a young man, just 35, but his production was clearly off in 1938. He batted just .295 with 29 home runs and 114 RBIs, solid numbers for most players, but his lowest production in years. In June 1938, he had played in his 2,000th consecutive game and the iron man streak would stretch to 2,130, ending on May 2, 1939. Gradual muscular deterioration caused by amytrophic lateral sclerosis had sapped Gehrig of his strength and, within two years, the disease would claim his life.

In the summer of 1939, the Hall of Fame was dedicated in Cooperstown, New York, where, if he didn't invent baseball, native Abner Doubleday did have some input in the game.

The first inductees elected by the Baseball Writers Association of America were Ty Cobb, Walter Johnson, Christy Mathewson, Babe Ruth and Honus Wagner— not a bad nucleus for a baseball shrine. None, however, was a unanimous choice, Cobb coming closest with 222 of a possible 226 votes. That first election established a tradition. No player since, regardless of how impeccable his credentials, has ever won unanimous election to the Hall of Fame.

Gehrig getting one of his three hits in a game against the Cleveland Indians in 1938.

Talkative Cubs catcher Charles "Gabby" Hartnett was named Most Valuable Player for 1935.

Charles Leo "Gabby" Hartnett at batting practice, 1938.

Lou Gehrig marking his 2,000th consecutive game at first base for the New York Yankees.

Babe Ruth, in street clothes at Yankee Stadium farewell for Lou Gehrig, July 4, 1939.

New York Mayor Fiorello LaGuardia (standing at right of microphones) was among the 60,000 fans who paid tribute to Lou Gehrig. In the infield are the Washington Senators and the New York Yankees, with the famous 1927 Yankees nearest the camera in a row at the right.

A tearful Lou Gehrig at Yankee Stadium tribute to the Iron Horse, whose record-breaking career was cut short by illness.

FIFTH INNING

5

INTO WAR AND OUT OF IT 1940–1949

As baseball turned into a new decade, war clouds had gathered over Europe. World events would have an enormous impact on baseball, but on Opening Day, 1940, America was still at peace and Cleveland's fire-balling Bob Feller celebrated the start of the new season by throwing a no-hitter at Chicago.

Feller had come out of the fields of Iowa, equipped with an awesome fastball, clocked at better than 100 miles per hour. In the final game of the 1938 season, with Hank Greenberg still two home runs shy of Babe Ruth's 60, he and the Tigers had the misfortune of running into Feller. The Indians' flame-thrower not only denied Greenberg any homers, but he struck out a record 18 Detroit hitters.

In 1939, Feller won 24 games for the Indians and, at age 21, he was the ace of the Cleveland staff, entrusted with the Opening Day assignment against the White Sox. He responded brilliantly, striking out eight and making a single Cleveland run stand up for the victory. It remains the only no-hitter ever pitched in a season opener.

Joe DiMaggio's many achievements include two league batting titles and three Most Valuable Player awards.

New stars were emerging as old ones passed from the scene. Joe DiMaggio had established himself in New York, winning the American League batting title in 1939 with .381 and repeating in 1940 at .352. In Boston, the Red Sox unveiled Ted Williams, who broke in by hitting .327 and leading the league with 145 RBIs in 1939, and then hitting .344 behind DiMaggio in 1940. The two would turn the season of 1941 into a most memorable baseball summer.

On May 15, 1941, DiMaggio had an RBI-single against Chicago's Eddie Smith. It was an otherwise innocuous hit and probably would have been lost to posterity except for what followed. For the next two months, for 56 consecutive games, DiMaggio produced at least one hit per game. There were three four-hit games, five three-hit games and 13 two-hit games during the streak. It was as if the Yankee center fielder had been transformed into a hitting machine, good game after game for one or more hits. There were 35 extra base hits, 15 of them home runs. There were 55 runs batted in and a stretch of 91 hits in 223 at-bats, a sizzling .408 pace.

The hitting streak finally ended on July 17 in Cleveland, when Al Smith and Jim Bagby stopped DiMaggio, holding him hitless in three official at-bats. Twice, he smashed shots at third baseman Ken Keltner and each time Keltner made the play and threw DiMaggio out. His final swing came in the eighth inning when he came to the plate with the bases loaded and one out. It was an ideal hitting situation, but Bagby escaped, getting DiMaggio to bang into a double play. The streak was over.

Stringing base hits together was nothing new for DiMaggio. In 1933 at San Francisco, he had hit in 61 straight games. And the interlude at Cleveland was distinctly temporary. He would hit safely in the next 17 games—meaning that over 74 games, Joe D. had been held without a hit only once. And that did not include the All-Star Game, in which he doubled.

Bob Feller came to the Cleveland Indians as an 18-year-old and became one of the game's great pitchers, winning 266 games and collecting 2,581 strikeouts.

In 1941, Joe DiMaggio hit safely in a record 56 consecutive games. Here, he collects a single in his 42nd game, breaking a record set by George Sisler in 1922.

The All-Star Game in 1941 belonged to Ted Williams. He had doubled in a run early and then, in the bottom of the ninth inning, with the American League trailing 5–4, he came to bat with two out and two men on base. With the count two balls and one strike, Claude Passeau fed the Boston slugger a fastball just above the knees. An inning earlier, Williams had struck out on that pitch. This time, he did not.

Williams connected, sending a long, high drive toward right field. The ball kept climbing, finally crashing into the third tier at Briggs Stadium for a three-run homer that gave the AL a pulsating 7–5 victory.

It was an entirely appropriate finish because DiMaggio's 56-game streak notwithstanding, Williams was baseball's hottest hitter in the summer of '41. He was hitting .435 in mid-June and steamed into September at right around the magic .400 figure. The Red Sox,

however, were out of the race, trailing New York by a fat 15 games as the season reached its final days. At that point, Williams was batting .3995—an average that when rounded off could give him baseball's first .400 season in 11 years. Since the last day's doubleheader at Philadelphia meant nothing in the standings, Boston manager Joe Cronin offered to give Williams the day off, protecting the .400 achievement. The slugger was having none of that. He would play both games. If he was going to hit .400, it would be with a bat in his hands, not hiding in the dugout.

In the opener, Williams singled in his first at-bat and homered in his next swing. He finished that game with four hits in five swings and then went 2-for-3 in the second game, finishing the season with a .406 average. It remains the last time a hitter batted over .400.

Ted Williams, the Red Sox' ''Splendid Splinter,'' was the last player to hit over .400 in a season. He hit .406 for the Bosox in 1941.

The Yankees' Joe DiMaggio (left) had something in common with both these Red Sox outfielders. He was a great hitter, like Ted Williams (center), and was Dom DiMaggio's brother.

Ted Williams (left) was an established young star and Babe Ruth (right) was nearing the end of his career when the two met in late 1943 to choose up sides for a batting contest.

Three DiMaggio brothers played major league baseball. Here, Dominic, a Red Sox rookie in 1940, got together with brother Joe, who was already established as a big league star.

Boston's "Lefty" Grove pitching against the Yankees in a 1941 game.

In the ninth inning of the fourth game of the 1941 World Series, Brooklyn catcher Mickey Owen (right) dropped a third strike, prolonging the inning and allowing the Yankees to take the lead and eventually win the game. Sliding home with the go-ahead run is Joe DiMaggio.

Fans argued about who was better—Ted Williams or Joe DiMaggio. A frequently heard rumor had the two traded for each other, but it never happened.

New York's string of three straight pennants had been interrupted by Detroit in 1940, but the Yankees returned to the World Series in 1941. And it turned into a Subway Series when, for the first time since 1920, Brooklyn took the National League flag. The Dodgers, equipped with a roster full of imported players, ended Cincinnati's two-year run at the top of the NL. The new names on the roster included catcher Mickey Owen from St. Louis, first baseman Dolph Camilli and pitcher Kirby Higbe from Philadelphia, second baseman Billy Herman from Chicago and shortstop Pee Wee Reese from Boston. They also signed free agent Pete Reiser, who would lead the league in hitting with a .341 average.

Trailing two games to one, the Dodgers were leading Game Four 4–3 in the ninth inning with relief ace Hugh Casey on the mound. The count went full on Tommy Henrich when Casey broke off a nasty pitch that acted suspiciously like a spitball. Henrich swung and missed but the ball bounded past Owen and Henrich made it safely to first base. Given a new life, the Yankees responded. DiMaggio singled and Charlie Keller followed with a double that chased two runs home. Bill Dickey walked and Joe Gordon followed with a double, giving New York a 7–4 victory.

The Yankees clinched the Series the next day and Mickey Owen had a permanent if not pleasant place in World Series history.

The New York Giants great Mel Ott playing "pepper" in the spring of 1941.

Two months after Owens' Series-turning passed ball, Japan bombed Pearl Harbor, plunging the United States into World War II. Suddenly, pennant races were secondary to the country's war effort. Within a year, the top players in the game had marched off to war, some to see combat, others in less dangerous roles; all, however, gone from major league rosters.

Judge Landis turned to President Franklin D. Roosevelt to ask how baseball could best serve the war effort. The President's advice was to carry on.

"I honestly feel it would be best for the country to keep baseball going," Roosevelt wrote the commissioner. "There will be fewer people unemployed and everybody will work longer hours and harder than ever before. And that means they ought to have a chance for recreation and for taking their minds off their work even more than before."

So baseball pressed ahead. With stars like DiMaggio, Greenberg, Williams, Feller and so many others either enlisting or drafted, teams filled their places with men who might otherwise not have had the chance to play in the big leagues. Sometimes, they weren't quite men, yet. Things got so tough in Cincinnati that in 1944, the Reds sent 15-year-old Joe Nuxhall out to pitch. He allowed two hits and walked five batters in two-thirds of an inning, his debut less than a rousing success.

Nuxhall left with a 67.50 earned run average but returned eight years later and, at the ripe old age of 23, began a more normal and certainly more productive major league career. Because of the demands of the war, however, he maintains a spot in baseball trivia—the youngest player ever to appear in a major league game.

The other side of the age coin were people like Babe Herman, who showed up in Brooklyn's outfield at age 42; Pepper Martin, resurrected by St. Louis at age 40; the Waner brothers, Paul and Lloyd, both playing well into their 40s; and Jimmie Foxx, used as a pitcher by the Philadelphia Phillies at age 38. Foxx might have been as good a pitcher as he was a hitter. He won his only decision and had a 1.59 ERA in nine games.

Typical of the manpower situation was the decision in 1945 of the St. Louis Browns to sign outfielder Pete Gray, whose credentials included batting .333 for Memphis of the Southern Association. Gray appeared in 77 games for the Browns, batting an unremarkable .218. What was remarkable, however, was that he did it with one arm.

The war years were a difficult time for baseball because of the manpower situation. The only team that was able to overcome the demands of the draft was the St. Louis Cardinals, who kept plugging in replacement players promoted from a vast farm system developed by Branch Rickey. Rickey was a former catcher, whose limited playing career—he hit .239 playing in parts of four seasons—gave no hint of the impact he would have on baseball. He had managed the Cardinals from 1919 to 1925 with limited success but then moved to the front office, where he found his niche. He masterminded construction of baseball's farm system network and the Cards flourished with five pennants in nine years from 1926 to 1934.

Babe Ruth, warming up before a batting exhibition at Yankee Stadium in 1942.

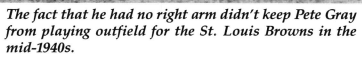

The fact that he had no right arm didn't keep Pete Gray from playing outfield for the St. Louis Browns in the mid-1940s.

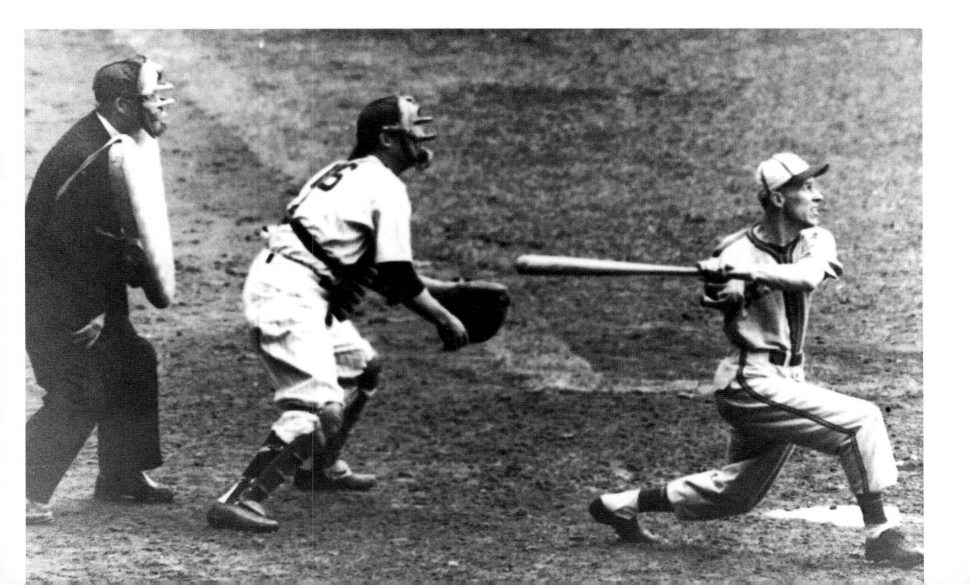

In 1942, the first year of the war, Brooklyn was sitting on a 10-game lead in August before the St. Louis Cardinals put on one of history's greatest stretch drives, winning 43 of the final 51 games to take the pennant by two games. The Cardinals were led by a slender left-handed hitter, who had given up pitching when he developed a sore arm. It turned out to be a most clever career move, for Stan Musial batted .315 that rookie year and won the first of his seven batting titles the next year when he batted .357.

The Cardinals would win four pennants in five years, getting big production from Musial; the Cooper brothers, catcher Walker and pitcher Mort; slick fielding shortstop Marty Marion; Whitey Kurowski; Terry Moore; Enos Slaughter; Harry Walker and others. Almost all of them were products of Rickey's far-flung farm system. They would flourish, however, without Rickey, who left St. Louis for Brooklyn when Dodger boss Larry MacPhail went off to war.

St. Louis celebrated its last-day pennant victory in 1942, beating the Yankees in five games, sweeping four straight after dropping the opener. New York had won eight straight World Series before the Cardinals ended that string. In a rematch a year later, the Yankees got their revenge, winning the title in five games for their seventh and final world championship under manager Joe McCarthy.

The Cardinals made it three straight pennants in 1944 and that flag was special because when the Browns won their first and only American League title on the last day of the season, it provided St. Louis with the host role for the entire World Series. There were no travel days in the schedule and all games were played in Sportsman's Park, owned by the Browns and leased by the Cardinals. It was a cozy situation.

The Browns lived up to their reputation, making 10 errors and batting a less than lusty .188 and losing the Series in six games. Only George McQuinn's .438 batting average saved the Browns from complete embarrassment.

Baseball Commissioner Kenesaw Mountain Landis helped the New York Yankees celebrate after they beat the St. Louis Cardinals in the 1943 World Series.

Branch Rickey signed star second baseman Joe ''Ducky''
Medwick to a 1939 St. Louis contract worth about
$18,000—a bargain by today's standards.

Three National League stars of the 1940s and '50s—(from
left) Enos Slaughter, Ralph Kiner, and Stan Musial—
before a game late in the 1949 season.

With the war winding down, players began returning from military service in 1945. Among the first to come back was Detroit slugger Hank Greenberg, appropriate since he was one of the first to leave in 1941. In his first game back, Greenberg smacked a home run and when the pennant race between Detroit and Washington came down to the season's final day, he clinched the flag in the most dramatic way imaginable—with a ninth inning grand slam home run.

Chicago interrupted the Cardinals' wartime reign on top of the National League, aided greatly by the mid-season acquisition from the Yankees of curve-balling Hank Borowy. The Cubs got 11 wins in half a season from Borowy and he shut the Tigers out in the Series opener. Greenberg's three-run homer helped Detroit even the Series but then Claude Passeau threw a one-hitter to give Chicago Game Three. Dizzy Trout evened the Series, 4–1, and then Greenberg drilled three doubles to help Detroit win Game Five. The Tigers wiped out a four-run deficit to tie Game Six but Borowy, working out of the bullpen, held Detroit hitless for four innings before the Cubs won in the 12th inning.

For Game Seven, Chicago manager Charlie Grimm went right back to Borowy, his third straight game on the mound. He had nothing left and was lifted after surrendering hits to the first three Detroit hitters. The score was 5–0 before Chicago ever got to bat and the Tigers went on to a 9–3 romp for the championship.

The Cardinals were back on top in 1946, but they had company. Brooklyn, reconstructed by Rickey, tied St. Louis for the National League pennant, both teams finishing the regular season with 96–58 records. That necessitated the first-ever pennant playoff and St. Louis took charge of that, winning two straight to nail down its fourth flag in five years. Waiting for the Cardinals in the World Series were the Boston Red Sox. It promised to be an intriguing matchup between Ted Williams, who hit .342 for the Bosox, and Stan Musial, who led the National League in six offensive categories, batting .365.

Hank Greenberg of the Detroit Tigers trying out a new position, the outfield, at spring training before the war. Rudy York was replacing him at first base.

Two of baseball's premier players: Boston Red Sox Ted Williams (left) and St. Louis Cardinal Stan Musial.

The teams struggled on even terms through six games and with the Series on the line, Game Seven was tied at 3-3 with St. Louis at bat in the bottom of the eighth inning. Enos Slaughter, playing with a broken elbow, opened the inning with a single. Two outs later, he was still anchored at first base. Then Harry Walker drilled a hit to left center. Slaughter was off with the crack of the bat. He dashed around second, heading for third as Leon Culberson recovered the ball. Culberson's relay went to shortstop Johnny Pesky as third base coach Mike Gonzalez tried to stop Slaughter there. Slaughter, however, was having none of that. He ran right through the stop sign. Pesky hesitated for a split second, never expecting the runner to try and score. His throw was late as Slaughter slid across the plate with the run that won the World Series.

The Cardinals beat the Red Sox in the 1946 World Series when Enos Slaughter scored from first base on Harry Walker's two-out single in the eighth inning of the final game.

The most significant event of the 1946 season, however, occurred not on the field but off it. In Brooklyn, Branch Rickey decided it was time that baseball ended its exclusion of black players. Until then, blacks had been segregated in their own leagues, their accomplishments not widely known. They were shunned by the majors strictly because of their race, an injustice that angered Rickey and one he set out to change. So, in 1946, he signed organized baseball's first black player, a former UCLA star named Jackie Robinson. Rickey sent Robinson to the Dodgers' Triple A farm club at Montreal where he won the International League batting title, hitting .349.

The Dodger braintrust in 1943 included manager Leo Durocher (left) and president Branch Rickey.

The Negro leagues provided the major leagues with many star ball players. One of the greatest was pitcher Leroy ''Satchel'' Paige, who played with the Kansas City Monarchs, here shaking hands with David Barnhill of the New York Cubans.

Leroy "Satchel" Paige was a star pitcher in the Negro leagues before making a name for himself in the major leagues.

Robinson had been carefully recruited by Rickey. The Dodger boss knew that the man he chose to break baseball's color line would have to be a special individual, capable of facing enormous pressure. He would have to be talented enough to excel on the field and controlled enough to ignore the harassment and hostility his presence almost certainly would trigger. Robinson had been a four-sport star at UCLA and an Army officer during World War II. He would turn out to be a brilliant choice.

Rickey could not introduce a black player unilaterally. A meeting of the owners was called, presided over by Happy Chandler, the former governor of Kentucky who became commissioner after the death of Judge Landis in 1944. Chandler's campaign slogan to get the commissioner's job was simple. He kept saying, "Ah love baseball," and that proved sufficient. Now, though, he was faced with a time bomb and the solution would require more than a down-home homily.

The 16 clubs voted on the issue and there were 15 opposed to Rickey's revolutionary idea. The matter would be decided in the end by Chandler and the commissioner offered a most logical solution: "If a black can fight for his country in Okinawa and Guadalcanal,

he can play organized baseball," he said. The issue was settled. Robinson could be signed by the Dodgers.

The year in Montreal was a warmup. Robinson excelled and on April 10, 1947, on the eve of a new season, the Dodgers distributed a one-sentence press release. It said: "The Brooklyn Dodgers today purchased the contract of Jackie Roosevelt Robinson from the Montreal Royals." One sentence that spoke volumes.

Robinson's promotion was not greeted warmly on a number of fronts, including his own clubhouse. There were pockets of resistance on the Dodgers but it was more virulent among other teams. Bench jockeys were merciless, holding back nothing as they rained abuse down on the rookie. There was even talk in St. Louis of a wholesale strike, a refusal to play Brooklyn if the Dodgers insisted on using a black man. Ford Frick, then president of the National League and later commissioner, issued a straightforward response to the Cardinals' threat:

"If you do this, you will be suspended from the league," Frick said. "I don't care if half the league strikes. . .This is the United States of America and one citizen has as much right to play as another."

A.B. ''Happy'' Chandler became the commissioner of baseball in 1945, after the death of Kenesaw Mountain Landis, who held the post for 24 years.

Jackie Robinson became the first black to play in the major leagues when he signed a contract with the Brooklyn Dodgers prior to the 1947 season.

The Dodgers starting infield for 1947.

So Robinson played, under the most difficult of circumstances. At one point, when the abuse became excessive, Dodger shortstop Pee Wee Reese, a native of Louisville, Kentucky, strolled over to Robinson and placed his arm around the black player's shoulder. It was a silent statement, an eloquent exhibition of support from one man to another.

Robinson played first base that season, batted .297, led the league with 29 stolen bases and was named Rookie of the Year. The Dodgers, with Burt Shotton replacing the suspended Leo Durocher as manager, beat the Cardinals by five games for the pennant and found their neighbors, the New York Yankees, waiting for them in the World Series.

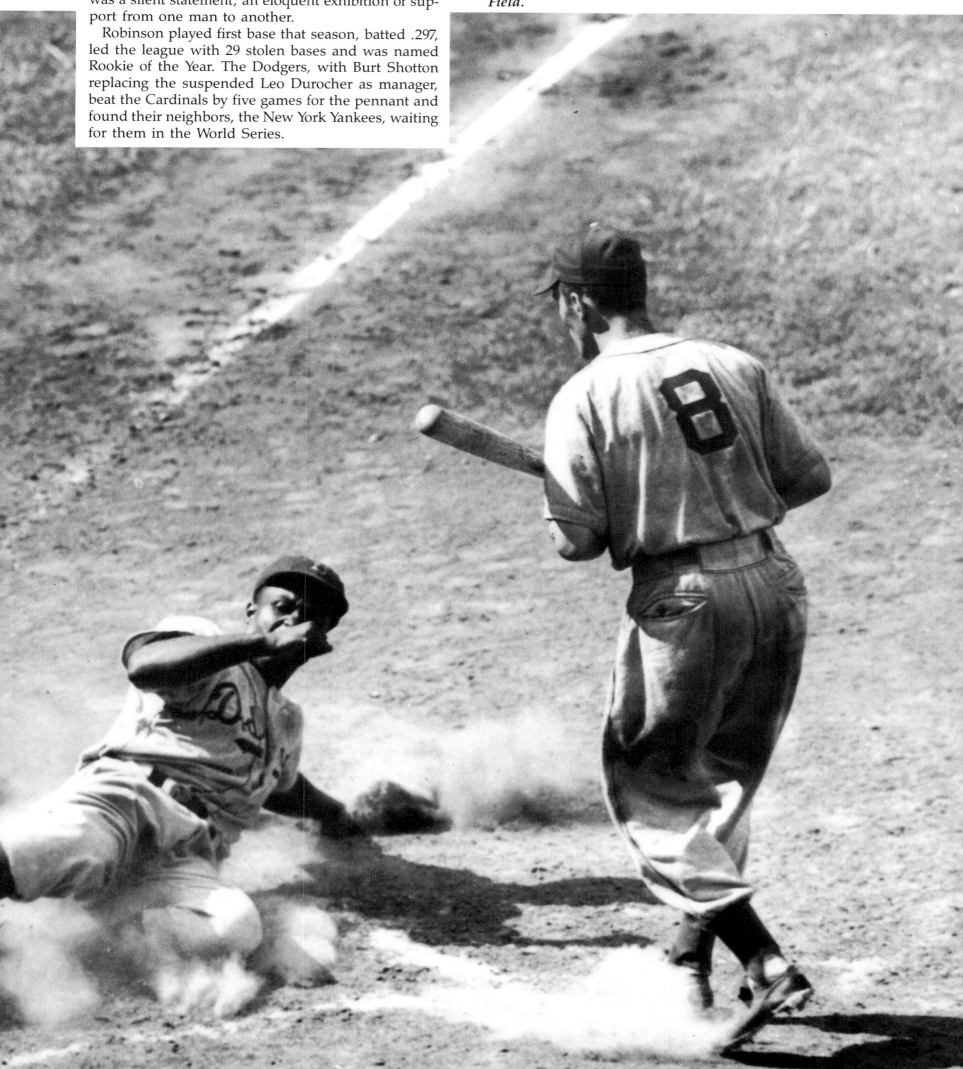

Brooklyn second baseman Jackie Robinson was a great base stealer, but he was out this time, attempting to steal home in a 1948 game against the Cubs at Wrigley Field.

Jackie Robinson was awarded a silver bat by National League President Ford C. Frick for being the league's 1949 batting champion with a .342 average.

Jackie Robinson was coming off a season that saw him win the National League batting championship and Most Valuable Player Award when club president Branch Rickey signed him to a 1950 contract.

*Brooklyn Dodgers second baseman Jackie Robinson was
awarded the National League's Most Valuable Player
Award in 1949.*

The Yankees won the first two games at home but Brooklyn took Game Three, despite the first pinch hit home run in World Series history, tagged by rookie catcher Yogi Berra. For Game Four, New York started Bill Bevens, a rather erratic right-hander who had struggled through a 7–13 season. On this day, however, Bevens was nearly unhittable.

No pitcher had ever thrown a no-hitter in World Series history but Bevens was flirting with one, carrying a 2–1 lead into the ninth inning. After Bruce Edwards flied out, Carl Furillo walked—the ninth base on balls Bevens had permitted. Spider Jorgensen fouled out and with the Dodgers down to their final out, pinch runner Al Gionfriddo took off for second on an attempted steal. If he had been out, Bevens would have had his no-hitter. But Berra's throw was late and Gionfriddo slid in safely. Now, with the tying run in scoring position, Yankee manager Bucky Harris elected to walk pinch hitter Pete Reiser intentionally, flouting the baseball adage that you never put the winning run on base.

Cookie Lavagetto was sent up to hit for Eddie Stanky and in one swing of his bat, Bevens' no-hitter and the Yankee victory evaporated. Lavagetto sent a double off the right field wall that chased home both runs and gave the Dodgers their victory. It was the last major league pitch hard luck Bill Bevens ever threw.

The Yankees recovered from that shock—as well as a brilliant running catch by Gionfriddo in Game Six that robbed Joe DiMaggio of a two-run triple—to defeat the Dodgers in seven games.

Encouraged by Robinson's success in Brooklyn, Cleveland owner Bill Veeck integrated the American League in 1948, signing outfielder Larry Doby. The young man arrived in the middle of a dandy pennant race between the Indians and Boston Red Sox, one destined to end in a tie, forcing the first playoff in the American League. Cleveland player-manager Lou Boudreau smashed two home runs and Ken Keltner had a three-run shot, leading the Indians to an 8–3 victory and a World Series date with the Boston Braves.

These were the Braves of "Spahn and Sain and pray for rain." The aces of the Boston staff were left-hander Warren Spahn, who would finish his career with 363 victories, and righty Johnny Sain, who led the league that year with 24 victories. Behind those two, the Braves used a potpourri of pitchers, a good enough group to get Boston home in first place, but not good enough to get them past the Indians. Cleveland took the Series in six games, its first World Championship in 28 years.

The Yankees were accustomed to winning and being limited to one World Series appearance in five years did not sit well with the brass. So, in 1949, New York imported a new manager to turn things around. Charles Dillon Stengel was something of a comical character, equipped with a rubbery face and scrambled syntax that left listeners scratching their heads. Casey also was a pretty good manager and he proved that immediately. It was no simple task, especially when New York reached the final weekend of the season still one game behind Boston with two games to play, both against the Red Sox.

It proved to be no problem for the Yankees. They wiped out a 4–0 deficit to win the first game on a late home run by Johnny Lindell, tying Boston for first place. The next day, behind the gritty pitching of Vic Raschi, New York won, 5–3, clinching the pennant.

Over in the other league, Brooklyn was locked in a tight race with St. Louis that also went down to the final day of the season. With a Cardinal victory already posted on the scoreboard and another playoff with the Cardinals beckoning if they lost, the Dodgers blew an early 5–0 lead against Philadelphia but then came back to win the game and the pennant, 9–7, in 10 innings.

The opening game of the World Series was a brilliant pitching duel between Don Newcombe and Allie Reynolds, settled by Tommy Henrich's leadoff home run in the bottom of the ninth inning that gave the Yankees a 1–0 victory. It was the closest Newcombe, an otherwise brilliant pitcher, ever came to a World Series win. The Dodgers won Game Two 1–0 on Preacher Roe's six-hitter, but the Yankees swept the next three for the title. It was Casey Stengel's first world championship, but it would not be his last.

Pee Wee Reese, star shortstop for the Dodgers as well as team captain, meets with club president Branch Rickey prior to the start of the 1949 World Series against the New York Yankees.

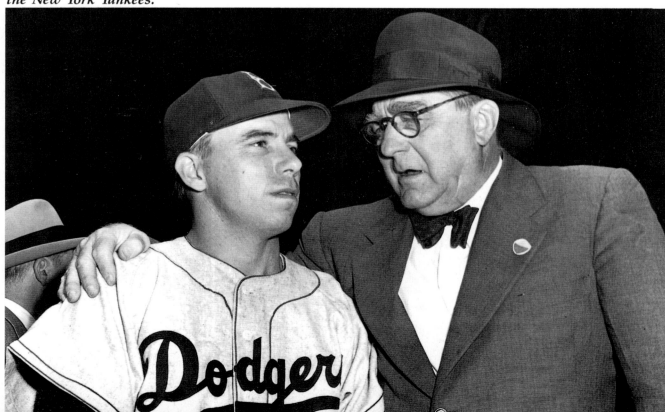

Casesy Stengel became famous as a manager, but it is sometimes overlooked that he was a pretty good player, too. He is shown here taking a practice cut in 1934.

SIXTH INNING

6

THE FABULOUS FIFTIES 1950–1959

It had been 35 years since the Philadelphia Phillies won the National League pennant, but in 1950 the club assembled a young, talented team that opened a big early lead and turned into the last 10 days of the season ahead by eight games. Then the Whiz Kids nearly went fizz.

By the time the Phillies got to Brooklyn for the final two games of the season, their lead over the Dodgers was down to two games. When Brooklyn won the first game 7–3, the pressure was really on the Phillies. With the pennant on the line, manager Eddie Sawyer handed the baseball to the ace of his staff, Robin Roberts, for his third start in five days, against Don Newcombe. Roberts had beaten Newcombe on Opening Day and now, six months later, they would face off again, this time for the flag.

The score was tied 1–1 into the ninth and the Dodgers had runners on first and second when Duke Snider singled. But Cal Abrams was thrown out at the plate by Richie Ashburn. Then Roberts squirmed out of trouble, retiring Carl Furillo and Gil Hodges with the bases loaded. When Dick Sisler hit a three-run homer in the

10th, the pennant belonged to Philadelphia.

The Phillies were no match for Stengel's Yankees in the World Series and were swept in four games, scoring just five runs.

At the end of the Series, an era ended in baseball when Connie Mack announced his retirement as manager of the Philadelphia A's, the franchise he founded and piloted from the time the American League was formed in 1901. Mack was 87, a throwback to the beginnings of modern baseball. He was a fixture on the A's bench, wearing a starched collar and straw hat years after they had gone out of fashion. Other managers were called "Skipper" by their players. The A's boss was always "Mr. Mack."

In baseball's executive suite, Commissioner Happy Chandler had accumulated his share of enemies among the owners and by mid-summer of 1951, he was gone. In September, Ford Frick, the president of the National League, was elected to succeed Chandler, the ex-governor who was a successful politician except in baseball circles.

By then, the National League was locked in an excit-

Mickey Mantle (right) with Yogi Berra.

Joe DiMaggio

ing pennant race. In August, Brooklyn was sitting on a 13½-game lead and seemed capable of cruising to the crown. But then their crosstown rivals, the New York Giants, started winning. With ex-Dodger manager Leo Durocher running the team, the Giants won 37 of their last 44 games to catch Brooklyn in the final weekend of the season. Only a brilliant individual show by Jackie Robinson—he made a game-saving catch in the 12th inning and then hit a game-winning home run in the 14th—saved Brooklyn's pennant hopes with a pulsating last-game victory over Philadelphia.

That sent the pennant race into a three-game playoff. New York won the opener 3–1, but the Dodgers roared back with a 10–0 romp in the second game. Brooklyn led the third and deciding game 4–1 as the Giants came to bat one last time in the bottom of the ninth. Hits by Alvin Dark, Don Mueller and Whitey Lockman made it 4–2 and brought Bobby Thomson to the plate for New York. Ralph Branca relieved Newcombe for the Dodgers and slipped a strike past Thomson. On the Giants' bench, the players moaned over a missed opportunity. The pitch had been in Thomson's wheelhouse. He had frozen on it. Certainly he wouldn't get that good a pitch to hit again.

Amazingly, however, he did. This time Thomson did not let it pass. He drilled a three-run homer into the lower deck in left field at the Polo Grounds, winning the pennant and setting off pandemonium. It was the dream ending to a dream race between two fierce opponents. And as Thomson circled the bases, celebrating the homer that would come to be known as "The Shot Heard 'Round the World," Robinson stood on the field, watching him, just to make sure he touched every one of them.

Joe DiMaggio, 1951.

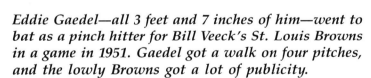

Eddie Gaedel—all 3 feet and 7 inches of him—went to bat as a pinch hitter for Bill Veeck's St. Louis Browns in a game in 1951. Gaedel got a walk on four pitches, and the lowly Browns got a lot of publicity.

October 3, 1951, became one of the most memorable days in baseball history when New York Giants outfielder Bobby Thomson—in the center of the mob with a hand on his head—hit a ninth inning come-from-behind three-run home run in the final playoff game against the Dodgers to give the Giants the National League pennant.

Waiting on deck when Thomson hit his home run was a frightened 20-year-old rookie who had energized the Giants' rush to overtake the Dodgers. Willie Mays had been promoted from the minors one month into the season to breathe new life into the team. In time, he would be part of a spirited debate among New York fans over the merits of the town's three center fielders. The talk of New York in the '50s was who was better— Willie Mays of the Giants, Mickey Mantle of the Yankees or Duke Snider of the Dodgers. The issue was never resolved to everyone's satifaction, but all three did wind up in the Hall of Fame.

Thomson's dramatic, pennant-winning home run made the World Series seem almost anti-climactic, although the Yankees' six-game victory was notable on a couple of fronts. First, it marked the departure from baseball of the great Joe DiMaggio. Hounded by nagging injuries that cut into his production, the graceful DiMaggio hit one last home run in the fourth game and then called it quits. His successor would be Mantle, but in the second game of the Series, the rookie tore up his right knee, the first of a string of injuries that dogged him through his career.

During the summer of '51, Bill Veeck, the showman owner of the St. Louis Browns, was becoming bored with his team's losing ways. Veeck was in baseball to have a little fun and watching those Browns was anything but that. So he decided to do something about it.

In the second game of an otherwise unremarkable August doubleheader against Detroit, Veeck ordered a pinch hitter for the pitcher. Not just any pinch hitter, you understand, but rather a specific one—Eddie Gaedel. This would be Gaedel's one and only appearance at the plate and he was under strict orders not to swing the bat. Swing it? He could hardly lift it, since he was just 3 feet, 7 inches tall.

The authorities were, of course, outraged at the idea of using a midget and moved quickly to prevent it from happening again. Veeck was satisfied, having had his laugh. And Gaedel departed—predictably—with a base on balls in his only trip to the plate.

Edwin "Duke" Snider was one of the most popular of the Brooklyn Dodgers of the 1950s. The Duke was a fleet-footed center fielder with plenty of home run power.

In 1952, the new baseball commissioner, Ford Frick, visited spring training camps, where he ran into St. Louis Cardinals star outfielder Stan Musial.

Some Brooklyn Dodger greats gathered at Ebbets Field to build a snowman after a snowstorm canceled an exhibition game in 1950. Pictured are (from left) Roy Campanella, Pee Wee Reese, the snowman, Gil Hodges, and Jackie Robinson.

If the Dodgers were deflated by the shock of Thomson's pennant-winning home run, it hardly showed. Brooklyn returned to the World Series in 1952 and 1953, losing each time to the Yankees, first in seven games, then in six. Those were the "Boys of Summer"—Gil Hodges, Jackie Robinson, Pee Wee Reese, Duke Snider, Carl Furillo, Roy Campanella, Don Newcombe, Carl Erskine. It was a potent lineup from top to bottom.

With DiMaggio gone, Mantle became the Yankees' center fielder and main power hitter. He, too, had help, from people like Hank Bauer, Gene Woodling, Yogi Berra and Phil Rizzuto, but Mantle clearly was the main cog in Casey Stengel's machine. In early 1953, he certified that status with a monster home run in Washington's Griffith Stadium that soared over the 55-foot-high left field fence and landed in a backyard across the street from the ballpark, 565 feet from home plate. It was a blunt statement of the power of this switch-hitting slugger from Oklahoma.

When Yankee center fielder Mickey Mantle came to the majors, he had Joe DiMaggio's spikes to fill. Mantle responded to the challenge with 536 career home runs and three Most Valuable Player awards.

When Brooklyn's Duke Snider hit his fourth home run in the 1952 World Series against the Yankees, he tied a record held by Babe Ruth and Lou Gehrig.

Ted Williams, 1956.

In 1951, Bob Feller of the Cleveland Indians became the first pitcher in major league history to throw three no-hitters.

For 50 years, through two world wars and the Depression, baseball had been stable with 16 franchises in place, thriving in good times, surviving in bad. That would change in 1953, when Boston Braves owner Lou Perini received permission to transfer his team to Milwaukee. The club had attracted just 281,000 fans the year before and Perini had decided that Boston could no longer support two teams. His move would signal the start of major mobility for franchises. Six months after Milwaukee got the Braves, Bill Veeck sold the St. Louis Browns to interests that would move the team to Baltimore and change its name to the Orioles.

The Yankees' World Series victories in 1952 and 1953 gave Casey Stengel's team a record five consecutive world championships. That string would end in 1954, a year in which New York won 103 games—more than it had in any of the previous five title years. It ended, however, because the Cleveland Indians won 111 games, second only to the 116 that the Chicago Cubs won in 1906.

These Indians were awesome. They were led by Bobby Avila, who won the batting championship with a .341 average, and Larry Doby, who led the league in home runs with 32 and runs batted in with 126. Early Wynn and Bob Lemon each won 23 games and the Tribe's pitching staff was so good that Bob Feller was the No.4 starter.

Casey Stengel, 1962.

A couple of Yankees, Phil Rizzuto and Billy Martin, celebrated the team's fifth consecutive world championship after they beat the Brooklyn Dodgers in the 1953 World Series.

Waiting for the Indians in the World Series were the New York Giants, viewed as heavy underdogs because Cleveland seemed to have so many answers. The opening game set the tone, however, leaving the Indians rather dumbstruck at a curious turn of events.

With the score tied at 2–2 in the eighth inning, Doby walked and Al Rosen singled. Don Liddle relieved for New York to face Vic Wertz, who already had three hits. Wertz connected and sent a towering drive to the deepest part of center field in the Polo Grounds. Willie Mays was off at the crack of the bat, running at full speed with his back to the plate. Unbelieveably, he overtook the ball, catching it over his left shoulder some 460 feet from home plate. The play cut the heart out of the Indians. Two innings later, Dusty Rhodes completed the surgery.

Rhodes was a spare part for the Giants and in the 10th inning of the Series opener, with two men on base, he pinch hit a lazy fly ball to right field. Bobby Avila at second base thought it was nothing more than a harmless pop fly and started back for the ball. He was still waiting for it when the pop fly caught the close-in seats in right field for a 260-foot home run.

Cleveland went into shock and the Giants swept the next three games for the world championship. Those Indians never quite figured out how a ball hit 460 feet could be an out and one hit 260 feet could be a home run. But that was the way it was in the oddly-shaped Polo Grounds.

Brooklyn had never won a World Series and the frustration was mounting, especially after four wipeouts in seven years by the hated Yankees. But the Dodgers were determined to keep trying until they got it right. In 1955, they did. The team soared in front at the start of the season, winning its first 10 games and sitting on a 22–2 record after one month. Brooklyn would win the pennant by 13½ games and when they got to the Series, sure enough, there were their old pals, the Yankees, waiting for them.

One of the greatest catches in baseball history was made by one of the game's greatest players, Willie Mays. It happened on New York's Polo Grounds in the opening game of the 1954 World Series between the Giants and the Indians. The luckless batter was Vic Wertz.

In 1955, Willie Mays hit 51 home runs for the New York Giants to tie a club record held by Johnny Mize and lead the league for the season.

It wasn't long after Jackie Robinson (left) broke base-ball's color barrier that other black stars began play-ing in the majors. Among the first were (from second left) Larry Doby, Don Newcombe, Luke Easter, and Roy Campanella.

Willie Mays, 1969.

Willie Mays hit 660 home runs during his illustrious career in the National League. He led the league in home runs four times, and twice won the Most Valuable Player award.

When Brooklyn's Jackie Robinson (No. 42) stole home, Yankee catcher Yogi Berra voiced his disagreement with umpire Bill Summers' call in the opening game of the 1955 World Series.

Getting there wasn't easy for Casey Stengel's team. They broke open a tight, four-team race by winning 17 of their final 23 games and finished three games in front of the Indians.

New York won the first two games of the Series at home but then Brooklyn took the next three. The Yankees tied the Series in Game Six, sending the teams into another winner-take-all showdown. The Dodgers had a rested Don Newcombe ready to pitch, but he had never been able to beat the Yankees. So manager Walt Alston turned the assignment over to Johnny Podres, a 23-year-old left-hander who had gone 9–10 during the regular season, but had won Game Three of the Se-

ries. Podres had the Yankees shut out going into the sixth inning when Billy Martin opened with a walk and Gil McDougald beat out a bunt. Now Yogi Berra was up and with Brooklyn's outfield playing the lefty swinger to pull the ball, Berra sliced a fly ball down the line in left. It seemed certain to fall until Sandy Amoros, a defensive replacemet who had just come into the game, came racing into the corner, glove outstretched. Amoros made the one-handed catch, wheeled and doubled McDougald off first base. The rally-buster got Podres over the hump and he completed the shutout, giving the Dodgers their first-ever title.

The 1956 All-Star Game was one of many in which Ted Williams, Yogi Berra and Mickey Mantle played for the American League.

Casey Stengel (left) and Walter Alston were opposing managers in the 1956 World Series. Both men made it into the Hall of Fame on the strength of their managerial success.

Mickey Mantle showing off the ball he hit 565 feet in Griffith Stadium on April 17th, 1953.

Mantle, who had won the home run title in 1955, continued his long ball barrage the next year. On Memorial Day, he hit his 19th and 20th of the season in a double-header sweep against Washington. The first one was a gigantic drive that missed by a matter of inches being the first fair ball ever hit out of Yankee Stadium. The ball smacked hit near the top of the decorative roof cornice above the third deck, some 117 feet above the ground.

It would be a Triple Crown year for Mantle, who led the league in batting (.353), home runs (52) and RBIs (130) and he took the Yankees to still another World Series, once more against Brooklyn, which survived a three-team battle with Milwaukee and Cincinnati to take another National League flag.

Yankee manager Casey Stengel was feted on his 66th birthday by the fans in his hometown of Kansas City, Missouri.

The Series was deadlocked at two games apiece and for Game Five, the Yankees pitched Don Larsen, who had been knocked out in the second inning of Game Two. Larsen was a different man on this day, though. Working with a no-windup delivery, he breezed through the Brooklyn lineup. In the second inning, Jackie Robinson ripped a shot off the glove of third baseman Andy Carey. But the ball ricocheted to Gil McDougald at short, who threw Robinson out. In the fifth, Mantle made a running catch on a drive by Gil Hodges. That was as close as the Dodgers came to a hit. Larsen's 97th pitch was taken for a called third strike by pinch hitter Dale Mitchell, completing the only no-hitter—and a perfect game, at that—in World Series history.

Two games later, the Yankees were world champions again, completing a remarkable stretch of 10 years during which they beat either the Giants or Dodgers six out of seven World Series. They were truly the kings of New York and soon, they were baseball's only team in the nation's largest city.

Yogi Berra shows his appreciation to Don Larsen.

On October 8, 1956, Don Larsen pitched the first and only perfect game in the World Series as he beat the Brooklyn Dodgers 2–0 for the New York Yankees.

Ted Williams (left) and Ralph Kiner were two of baseball's most feared sluggers in the 1940s and '50s.

Duke Snider, 1963.

Four of a vanished breed—the .400 hitter—at an Old Timers' game at Yankee Stadium in 1958. From left, they are Bill Terry, Ted Williams, Rogers Hornsby and George Sisler.

In 1955, Stan Musial became only the 12th player in baseball history to collect 300 or more career home runs.

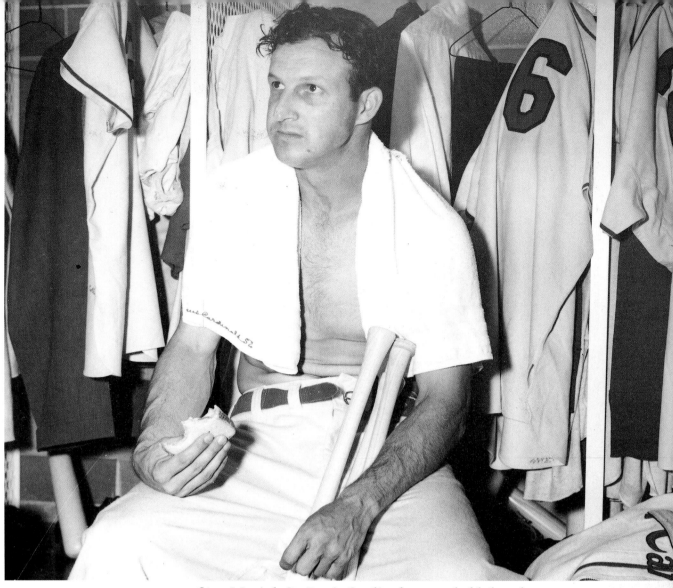

Stan Musial, St. Louis Cardinals great, held three bats after a 1954 game in which he hit three home runs. His familiar uniform No. 6 hangs behind him.

Missouri Governor James T. Blair presenting Stan Musial with a special license plate to honor the Cardinals great's 3,000th career base hit.
Another member of the 3,000-hit club, Tris Speaker (left) was on hand.

In 1959, Pittsburgh Pirates pitcher Harvey Haddix pitched 12 perfect innings against the Milwaukee Braves—and lost 1–0 in the 13th inning.

The Philadelphia A's had followed the lead of the Boston Braves and moved west in 1955, settling in Kansas City. With the St. Louis Browns relocated in Baltimore, baseball was experiencing a severe case of wanderlust and it surfaced next in Brooklyn, where owner Walter O'Malley was unhappy with the limited capacity of Ebbets Field. O'Malley started looking west—far west—and decided that Los Angeles would make a great home for the Dodgers. But the National League would not accept a single team on the West Coast. For O'Malley to move, he had to find somebody to go with him. That somebody turned out to be Horace Stoneham and the Giants.

The news hit New York like a thunderbolt. Instead of three teams, the city would have just one—the Yankees. The National League was leaving town and changing the baseball map dramatically.

If the Dodgers and Giants needed encouragement for their bold moves, they needed only to look at Milwaukee. The Braves were a box office smash, winning the National League pennant as Warren Spahn won 20 games for the eighth time. The bulk of the Braves' attack came from a young outfielder who led the league with 44 home runs and 132 RBIs. More would be heard later from Henry Aaron.

The Yankees won their eighth pennant in nine years but they could not halt Milwaukee's magic. The Braves took the World Series in seven games with Lew Burdette winning three of them, including the clincher on a shutout.

The transfer of the Giants and Dodgers was a roaring success financially. San Francisco, playing in tiny Seals Stadium, whose 23,000 capacity was 10,000 less than Ebbets Field held, attracted nearly 1.3 million fans. The Dodgers drew more than 1.8 million playing in a minor league park in Los Angeles. O'Malley's vision of the California pot of gold proved accurate and that proved particularly so for the Dodgers after they moved into a brand new stadium.

The Braves continued to flourish and won another National League flag. The Yankees were back in the World Series again, bent on revenge. When Milwaukee won three of the first four games, it shoved New York in a deep hole. But the Yankees climbed out, winning the last three games and becoming the first team since the 1925 to come back from a 1–3 deficit and win the World Series.

Until 1959, perhaps the most remarkable game ever pitched was the double no-hitter that Jim Vaughn and Fred Toney threw at each other in 1917. Or maybe it was Ernie Shore's 26-out perfect game after he relieved Babe Ruth in that same year. Or perhaps the no-hitter Bobo Holloman threw in his first major league start in 1953. On May 26, 1959, however, Harvey Haddix topped them all.

Haddix was a smallish left-hander who had won 20 games for St. Louis in 1953 but then bounced to Philadelphia, Cincinnati and Pittsburgh. He was in the middle of an otherwise unremarkable career when he wrote baseball history with a perfect game that ended less than perfectly.

For 12 innings against Milwaukee that night, Haddix did not allow a baserunner. Thirty-six Braves came up and 36 Braves went down. Never had a pitcher thrown a perfect game for longer than nine innings. Never had a pitcher taken a no-hitter past 11 innings. Now Haddix was perfect for 12. And the game was scoreless.

Felix Mantilla led off the 13th for the Braves and reached base when third baseman Don Hoak made a low throw on his ground ball. Eddie Mathews sacrificed Mantilla to second and then Hank Aaron was given an intentional walk. Joe Adcock was the next batter and he sent a drive over the wall in left field for Milwaukee's only hit of the game. In some basepath confusion, Adcock passed Aaron and was credited only with a double instead of a home run. It did not matter to Haddix, who had pitched what was the greatest game in history—and lost.

SEVENTH INNING

A DECADE OF EXPANSION 1960–1969

If Harvey Haddix' imperfect game in 1959 was the landmark pitching performance in baseball history, then two home runs hit the next year might be candidates for the most memorable long balls ever hit. The first came in a meaningless end of the season game for a seventh place team; the other in the classic drama of the last of the ninth inning in the seventh game of the World Series.

It was a dreary season for the Boston Red Sox, struggling to a 65–89 record, 32 games behind the New York Yankees. And, at age 42, it was the last year for the great Ted Williams. Twice, Williams' brilliant career had been interrupted by war. He lost three seasons during World War II and then the better part of two more when he was recalled to duty during the Korean conflict. Still, he had been one of the game's greatest hitters, winning six batting titles including the 1957 crown when, at age 39, he batted .388. There had been six RBI titles and four home run crowns and now he was winding down.

Williams had always been as controversial off the field as he was great on it. There had been an ugly episode

Harmon Killebrew.

in 1956 when he was fined $5,000 for spitting in the direction of fans who booed him after a misplay. There was a continuing feud with Boston newspapermen. Now, though, Williams would go out in style.

In his final major league at-bat, Williams hit a dramatic home run at Fenway Park, the 521st of his magnificent career. He circled the bases matter-of-factly, never acknowledging the standing ovation from the crowd, never tipping his hat in farewell, never coming out of the dugout for a curtain call. It was as if he were in too much of a hurry for such theatrics. There were fish to be caught and no time to be wasted getting to them.

Pittsburgh had not been to the World Series since 1927 when the Pirates watched in awe as the Yankees' Murderer's Row swept them in four games. Those Pirates should have seen these Yankees. New York came into the 1960 World Series loaded for bear and they did a number on Pittsburgh. The modern Yankees set Series records with 55 runs scored, 91 hits, 27 extra base hits and a lusty .338 team batting average. They also lost in seven games.

The problem was that the Yankee punch was concentrated and not distributed throughout the Series. After losing the opener 6–4, the Yankees won the next two games 16–3 and 10–0. But when Pittsburgh won the next two games 3–2 and 5–2, the Pirates were in position to take the title. Game Six was another Yankee romp, this time 12–0 as Whitey Ford threw his second shutout of the Series.

Below, at right: Ted Williams ''hung 'em up'' at the end of the 1960 season after an illustrious career that saw him win six batting championships and two Most Valuable Player awards.

Below: The season was under way in 1952 when Ted Williams turned in his Red Sox uniform for one from the Marine Corps.

Whitey Ford, New York Yankees star lefthander. His career 2.74 ERA is among the best in history of the game.

Ted Williams hit his 500th career home run in 1960, toward the end of his brilliant career. At the time, he was only the fourth player to reach the 500-home-run mark.

In Game Seven, New York wiped out an early 4–0 Pirate lead to go ahead 7–4. But Pittsburgh came back in the bottom of the eighth, their rally fueled when a double play grounder to Tony Kubek took a bad hop and hit the Yankee shortstop in the throat. Before they were done, the Pirates had scored five runs and were three outs away from the title.

But the Yankees rallied for two runs in the ninth to tie the score. Now it would be sudden death and the Yankees were the ones who succumbed.

Bill Mazeroski was Pittsburgh's first hitter in the bottom of the ninth. He was a solid second baseman, better known for his glove than his bat. Ralph Terry relieved for New York and his second pitch was right down Maz's alley. He sent the ball out to left field and Yogi Berra went to the base of the vine-covered wall at Forbes Field. Then Berra looked up and watched the ball drop over the fence—the first time a World Series ended with the drama of a home run.

The 1960 World Series was decided with a dramatic seventh game, ninth inning home run off the bat of second baseman Bill Mazeroski to give the Pittsburgh Pirates the World Championship.

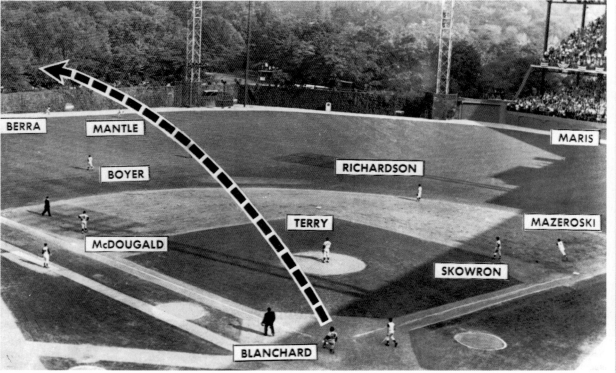

Mazeroski's shot also signaled another significant end. Casey Stengel's bosses in New York decided that after 12 years in which he won 10 pennants and seven world championships, it was time for the 71-year-old manager to retire. Stengel chose to describe the parting in less genteel terms, announcing that he had been fired. He would not be gone very long, though.

Stengel's successor in New York would be Ralph Houk, a longtime third string catcher whose playing career had been limited to 91 games over eight years. In 1961, he would oversee a record-shattering barrage of home runs, including one that would break one of baseball's most cherished records.

Roger Maris had been traded to New York before the 1960 season in one of those multi-player swaps the Yankees arranged so frequently with Kansas City. He had smashed 39 home runs, one back of league leader Mickey Mantle. The next year, the same two Yankee sluggers would stage another torrid power show. Throughout the summer, they punctuated a lusty long ball Yankee attack with fistfuls of home runs, as both made baseball's most serious run at Babe Ruth's record of 60 homers in a season.

The M and M boys, Roger Maris (left) and Mickey Mantle, in 1961.

Diagram showing flight of Mickey Mantle's home run in the bottom of the 11th inning against Kansas City on May 23, 1963. It missed by six feet being the first fair ball hit out of Yankee Stadium.

Mickey Mantle at bat.

But 1961 was a unique year. The departure of the Dodgers and Giants for the West Coast had touched off a demand to restore at least one new team to New York. And if the major leagues weren't willing to make that accommodation, well, there were other solutions, like a new league. Branch Rickey, always interested in new challenges, was putting together the Continental League, designed to provide a viable alternative for cities without teams—and some with them, like New York. Baseball moved quickly to cut the Continentals off at the pass, announcing expansion that would satisfy the need for more teams. The move would come in two stages, first two new teams for the American League in 1961, then two for the National League in 1962. Expansion would require extending the traditional 154-game schedule to 162. Ruth had hit his 60 homers in 154 games. What if his record were broken in the eight extra games?

Commissioner Ford Frick came up with a controversial solution—the asterisk, which would be appended to the home run record if it were broken in more than the 154 games that Ruth used. Frick's answer satisfied no one, but few people had time to think about it as through the summer, the home run race between the two Yankee teammates heated up. Two weeks into September, Maris was three home runs ahead, 56–53, with 18 games to play. And then the race abruptly ended. Mantle received an injection for a head cold. He developed an abscess on his hip, wound up in the hospital and managed just one more home run the rest of the way. Maris would complete the Ruth race alone. He hit No. 60 in the Yankees' 159th game and then broke the record in the final game of the season, actually New York's 163rd because the team had played one tie. Maris, however, played in only 161.

And Frick's asterisk? It was lost to posterity. The record book lists separate lines for 154-game seasons and 162-game seasons.

In the final game of the 1961 season, the Yankees' Roger Maris hit his 61st home run to break Babe Ruth's single-season home run record.

Maris and Mantle were just the beginning of the Yankee power show. Houk had three catchers—Berra, Elston Howard and Johnny Blanchard—and found enough playing time for them to get 64 homers out of the trio. First baseman Bill Skowron had 28 homers and the team finished with a record 240 home runs. Was that a function of the longer season? Well, the 154-game record was 221. And the Ruth-Gehrig Murderer's Row Yankees of 1927 hit just 158.

In the World Series, a bad year for Babe Ruth got worse. After Maris had broken the Babe's record of 60 homers, Whitey Ford cracked Ruth's mark of 29 2/3 consecutive shutout innings pitched in World Series play. Ford threw a two-hit shutout in the Series opener against Cincinnati. Following his two shutouts of Pittsburgh in the 1960 Series, it gave him 27 straight score-

Detroit Tigers outfielder Al Kaline in 1958.

Al Kaline (center) looking bug-eyed at the bat held by teammate Norm Cash and Harmon Killebrew of the Minnesota Twins before a game in July 1962.

less innings. He increased the total to 32 with five shutout innings in Game Four before a foot injury forced him out of the game. So, in the space of a week, two of Ruth's most spectacular records fell, one after 34 years, the other after 43 years.

The Yankees won the world championship in five games, but they were about to get company in New York. The American League expansion in 1961 had transferred Calvin Griffth's Washington Senators to Minneapolis and replaced them with a new Washington franchise, while also adding a team in Los Angeles. In 1962, it was the National League's turn and the new teams went to Houston and New York, where the new manager would be a resurrected Casey Stengel, now two years older than he had been when the Yankees cited his advancing years as a reason for his retirement.

Harmon Killebrew.

Twins' slugger Harmon Killebrew at work against the Washington Senators in 1962.

For Stengel, the job with the newly minted team represented a personal New York City grand slam. He had played for and/or managed each of the town's other franchises. But nothing he had done with the Giants, Dodgers and Yankees could have prepared him for what he found with the expansion team.

The 1962 Mets weren't bad. They were terrible. They found the most remarkable ways to lose games. They would lose a record 120 times in their first year, adding a few wrinkles to Stengel's already well-furrowed brow. The symbol of their futility was a journeyman first baseman named Marv Throneberry, who seemed to have a knack for misadventure. Once, Throneberry hit a ball that fell safely and enabled him to reach third base. On

an appeal play, he was declared out for failing to touch second. Stengel, outraged at this turn of events, charged out of the dugout to argue the call. Before he reached the umpires, the old man was intercepted by first base coach Cookie Lavagetto.

"Forget it, Case," Lavagetto advised the manager. "He didn't touch first, either."

While the Mets were floundering, their New York ancestors were flourishing. The Giants and Dodgers finished tied for the National League pennant and went

In 1965, Sandy Koufax became the first major league pitcher to hurl four no-hitters when he beat the Chicago Cubs with a perfect game.

into a three-game playoff that had remarkable similarities to the one they had engaged in 11 years earlier in New York. Once again, the Giants won the pennant, once again with a stirring ninth inning rally that wiped out a Dodger lead, once again earning a World Series date with the Yankees. Trailing 4–2 going into the top of the ninth, San Francisco bunched two singles, four walks, a wild pitch and an error into four runs for the pennant-winning rally. It lacked the dramatic impact of Bobby Thomson's home run but the result was the same, a Giant pennant.

The Series stretched seven games and in the bottom of the ninth in Game Seven, Willie McCovey was at bat with runners at second and third, two out and the Gi-

ants trailing, 1–0. McCovey was one of the Giants' most feared sluggers, and facing him was Ralph Terry, the man who had been victimized by Bill Mazeroski's Series-winning homer two years earlier. This time, fate was kinder to Terry. McCovey hit a bullet, a line drive right at second baseman Bobby Richardson to end the Series. A couple of feet either way, and the ball would have been past Richardson, allowing the tying and winning runs to score for San Francisco. It was that close.

Just as they had the first time they lost a pennant playoff to the Giants, the Dodgers staged an immediate recovery the very next year, a task simplified by the emergence of Sandy Koufax.

The Dodger's Sandy Koufax set a record for strikeouts in a World Series game when he fanned 15 New York Yankees in Game One of the 1963 Series.

Left handed pitcher Warren Spahn showing off uniforms indicating the 301st win of his career to Eddie Mathews Jr. in 1967.

Sandy Koufax.

Signed as a bonus baby, his development was retarded by wildness and a lack of opportunity to pitch on a team that was annually in contention. But when Koufax finally got his chance, he flourished. He harnessed his control, developed a wicked curve to go with an explosive fastball and became almost unhittable. He won 18 games in 1961 when he led the league with 269 strikeouts. Two years later, he took Los Angeles to a world championship, going 25–5 with a 1.88 earned run average, and beating the Yankees twice in the Dodgers' World Series sweep of New York.

As Koufax was emerging, two other great stars were reaching the end. Warren Spahn won 23 games in 1963, tying Christy Mathewson's record with his 13th 20-victory season. He finished the year with 350 wins and would manage just 13 more over the next two seasons before retiring. At the same time, Stan Musial called it quits, leaving with seven batting titles and a career .331 batting average.

Stan ''The Man'' Musial showing batting form in his 10,000th at-bat.

Within three weeks in the summer of 1964, the Mets certified their place as one of baseball's more curious teams. On Memorial Day, New York dropped a doubleheader to San Francisco, an unremarkable accomplishment considering the team's level of achievement in those days. What made it special was that the second game stretched through 23 innings and 7 hours, 23 minutes. It was the longest game in time elapsed in major league history and, combined with the first game, completed the longest doubleheader—9 hours, 52 minutes—in history. It was in the midst of a 10-inning relief stint for the Giants that Gaylord Perry said he began fooling around with the long-banned spitball. Perry would refine the technique and ride it to 314 career victories.

Three weeks after the 23-inning marathon, Stengel's Mets must have still been worn out. Facing Jim Bunning of Philadelphia, they failed to manage a single base-runner. Bunning's masterpiece was the eighth perfect game in history and made him the first pitcher in the game's modern era (since 1901) to throw a no-hitter in each league.

Bunning's Phillies seemed well on their way to the National League pennant, leading by 6½ games with 12 to play. But Philadelphia ran out of pitching and lost

Sandy Koufax won three Cy Young awards, including one in 1963, when he was also voted the National League's Most Valuable Player.

10 in a row, allowing St. Louis to sneak by and claim the flag. It was quite a recovery by the Cardinals who had struggled early, triggering rumors that manager Johnny Keane would be dismissed.

In New York, Yogi Berra had replaced Ralph Houk as manager of the Yankees and survived some rocky times to pilot the team to a fifth straight pennant. It was the 29th flag in 44 years for baseball's most successful franchise. And it marked the end of the Yankee dynasty.

In the Series, another Babe Ruth record fell when Mickey Mantle smashed three home runs, pushing his career total to 18. It was not good enough, however, to prevent the Cardinals from winning the world championship in seven games. That was not nearly as shocking as what happened in the next week.

Berra was fired. Keane quit. The two World Series managers were out of their jobs—but not for long. The Yankees, seeking a new skipper, looked around and decided a guy with World Series credentials would be perfect. So they hired Keane to manage the team he had just beaten.

That same week, the Braves' honeymoon in Milwaukee officially came to an end when the team declared its intention to move to Atlanta. The league approved the transfer for 1966, creating a lame duck season for the club in Milwaukee.

Headed by Koufax, pitchers were beginning to alter the balance of the game. For four consecutive years, Koufax threw no-hitters, punctuating the string with a perfect game against the Chicago Cubs September 10, 1965. He won 26 games that season, struck out 382 hitters and had a 2.04 ERA to win his fourth of five straight ERA crowns. He would go 27–9 the next year with a 1.73 ERA before an arthritic condition cut his career short at age 31.

Koufax pitched a pair of shutouts, the second on two days rest, as the Dodgers beat Minnesota in seven games to win the 1965 World Series. Los Angeles was back in the Series a year later but this time consecutive shutouts by Jim Palmer, Wally Bunker and Dave McNally gave the Baltimore Orioles a four-game sweep. The Dodgers batted .142, managing just 17 hits in the four games.

Pitcher Sandy Koufax and catcher John Roseboro celebrating the 1963 World Series win over the New York Yankees in four straight. Koufax won the first and fourth games.

Don Drysdale.

Don Drysdale of the Los Angeles Dodgers.

Jim Hunter.

The perfect ending is reflected in the smile of Jim ''Catfish'' Hunter after pitching a perfect game against the Minnesota Twins in 1968.

Batting averages were sagging and pitchers were dominating. The slumps were especially evident during the All-Star Games. The Nationals won a 10-inning battle 2–1 in 1966 with each team managing just six hits. A year later, the teams battled 15 innings and set a record with 30 strikeouts before Tony Perez' home run won it for the NL, 2–1. In 1968, the game's only run scored in the first inning when Willie Mays singled, took second on an error, advanced to third on a wild pitch and scored on a double play.

Catfish Hunter pitched a perfect game in May 1968. A month later, Don Drysdale completed a record scoreless string of 58 2/3 innings, breaking Walter Johnson's record of 56 innings. Denny McLain won 31 games, the first pitcher to reach 30 wins since Dizzy Dean did it in 1934. Bob Gibson posted a 1.12 earned run average, the lowest mark since 1914. Carl Yastrzemski won the American League batting title with a .301 average. The absence of offense was evident everywhere and baseball's policy-makers acted to restore the delicate balance between pitching and hitting. The pitching mound was lowered and the strike zone reduced.

In 1968, righthander Denny McLain of the Detroit Tigers became the first pitcher to reach the 30-win mark in a season since Dizzy Dean did it in 1934.

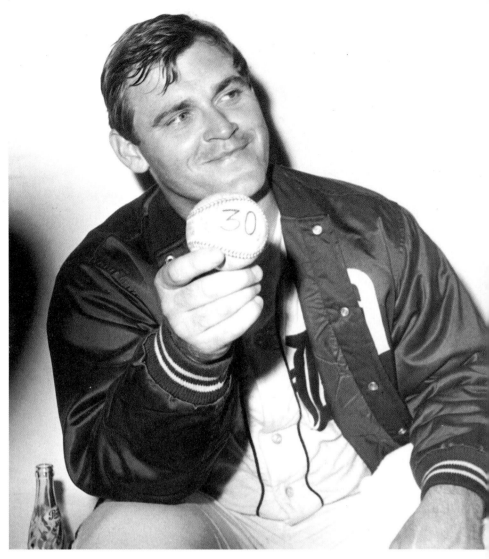

Don Drysdale making his first appearance in the 1963 World Series against the Yankees.

The Pirates' Roberto Clemente was a star in the field as well as at bat. He collected exactly 3,000 hits in his career and won four National League batting titles.

In 1968, Denny McLain won 31 games for the World Champion Detroit Tigers as well as the Cy Young and Most Valuable Player awards.

Carl Yastrzemski.

Yaz' batting championship was his second straight. In 1967, he had captured the Triple Crown and led Boston to its first flag in 21 years. This one was a shocker because the Red Sox had finished an undistinguished ninth the year before and were hardly expected to contend. They took St. Louis to seven games in the World Series before Bob Gibson's third victory sealed the championship. A year later, the Cardinals were back in the Series again. Gibson struck out 17 Detroit batters to set a record in the opener and St. Louis won three of the first four games. But the Tigers clawed back and with Gibson and Mickey Lolich each shooting for a third victory, Detroit took the Series in seven games.

Baseball moved into a new era in 1969, adding four expansion teams. The American League got a replacement team in Kansas City for the A's, who had moved to Oakland, and a club in Seattle. NL teams were placed in Montreal—the first franchise outside the United States—and San Diego. Each league would be divided into six-team East and West divisions, creating four regular season champions and a playoff each year to determine the World Series opponents.

It was a major change in the scheme of things and it was punctuated by one of the winners in that first year of divisional play. If the Red Sox' pennant in 1967 was a shocker, it was just an appetizer for 1969 when the perennial doormat Mets rose up to win for the first time. New York won the division, the pennant and then, perhaps most shockingly, the World Series, beating Baltimore, which won 109 games during the regular season but could not solve the Met magic in the Series.

Bob Gibson eyeing the champagne after his three-hit 7–2 victory over the Boston Red Sox to win the 1967 World Series.

Bob Gibson firing away for the St. Louis Cardinals in the fifth game of the 1964 World Series

EIGHTH INNING

8

BREAKING THE BANK 1970–1979

Ford Frick served as commissioner of baseball for 14 years, his administration known primarily for settling problems by declaring, "That's a league matter." When he retired in 1965, the owners chose as his successor a rather anonymous retired Air Force general named William Eckert, whose selection raised some eyebrows. "My God," one newsman exclaimed. "They've named the unknown soldier."

Eckert's low profile was in sharp contrast to baseball's first three commissioners, Kenesaw Mountain Landis, Happy Chandler and Frick, and within four years, the owners decided they had made a mistake and summarily dismissed him. The new commissioner would be a known commodity, selected from within baseball's inner circle. Bowie Kuhn was a Wall Street attorney who had served for many years as National League counsel. Kuhn would hold the commissioner's office for 15 years, steering the sport through some tumultuous times.

The Yankees had flourished by scouting and signing the best young talent, always capable of outbidding the competition for the players they wanted. But baseball decided there was something patently unfair about that system by which the rich always got richer. So the universal amateur draft was introduced with teams claiming free agent players one at a time in the reverse order of the previous season's standings. That did two things. It helped the have-nots get healthy and it signalled the end of the Yankee dynasty. For a dozen years, New York was an also-ran in the American League while other teams took a turn at the top. Baltimore was first.

The World Series loss to the Mets in 1969 brought the Orioles back with some extra resolve the next year. Baltimore won 108 games in the regular season and wasn't about to waste that accomplishment in the postseason. The Birds beat Minnesota in the playoffs and then dispatched a very good Cincinnati team in just five games, riding a spectacular defensive show by third baseman Brooks Robinson to the title. Lee May, one of the Reds' sluggers who was robbed regularly by Robinson, called the Oriole third baseman Hoover "because he's like a vacuum cleaner." The Orioles had four 20-game winners the next season, riding the consistent pitching of

Johnny Bench.

Jim Palmer, Dave McNally, Mike Cuellar and Pat Dobson to another American League East title. They beat an emerging Oakland team in the playoffs and then met Pittsburgh in the World Series. After Baltimore won the first two games at home, baseball tried a little experiment, scheduling Game Three at night. When the contest attracted a home audience of 61 million fans, night games in the World Series were here to stay.

Roberto Clemente had played with distinction for 17 years but only once, in 1960, did he have the postseason spotlight on him. Now, the Pittsburgh right fielder made the most of his second Series. Almost entirely on his own will power, Clemente brought the Pirates back and Pittsburgh went on to win the Series in seven games as he batted .414 and intimidated the Orioles with his running and throwing. A year later, he collected his 3,000th hit and then died tragically while on a rescue mission for flood victims in Nicaragua.

Roberto Clemente.

Bowie Kuhn.

Dave McNally.

Roberto Clemente, Pirate rightfielder, hit a home run in the seventh game of the 1971 World Series against Baltimore. Clemente was voted the World Series Most Valuable Player.

In 20 seasons, Tom Seaver won 311 games, including 61 shutouts. He struck out 3,640 batters, third best in baseball history.

Three of the San Francisco Giants' big stars—(from left) Willie Mays, Juan Marichal and Willie McCovey—were among the game's highest-salaried players in 1970, when each made over $100,000 a season.

Lefty Dave McNally's third-game victory over the Cincinnati Reds helped the Orioles become the 1970 world champions in five games.

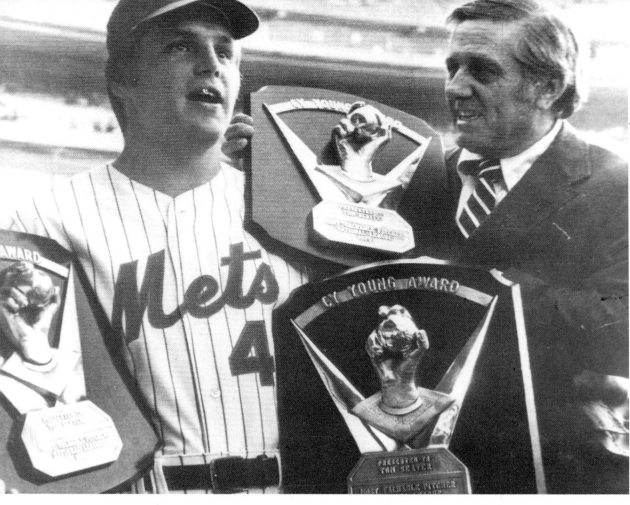

Mets' pitcher Tom Seaver won the Cy Young awards in 1969, 1973, and 1975.

Willie Stargell of the Pirates scored in the eighth inning of the seventh game of the 1971 World Series. It proved to be the winning run, as the Pirates beat the Baltimore Orioles 2–1 to become world champions.

Among the awards received by Frank Robinson in 1966 were the Babe Ruth Crown, a bowl in recognition of his winning baseball's Triple Crown, and a Sports magazine plaque honoring him as the year's top baseball player. Robinson also won the American League MVP and was MVP of the World Series.

Frank Robinson hit 586 home runs to place him fourth on the all-time list.

Ernie Banks.

In 1970, Cubs first baseman Ernie Banks joined an elite group of baseball players when he hit his 500th career home run.

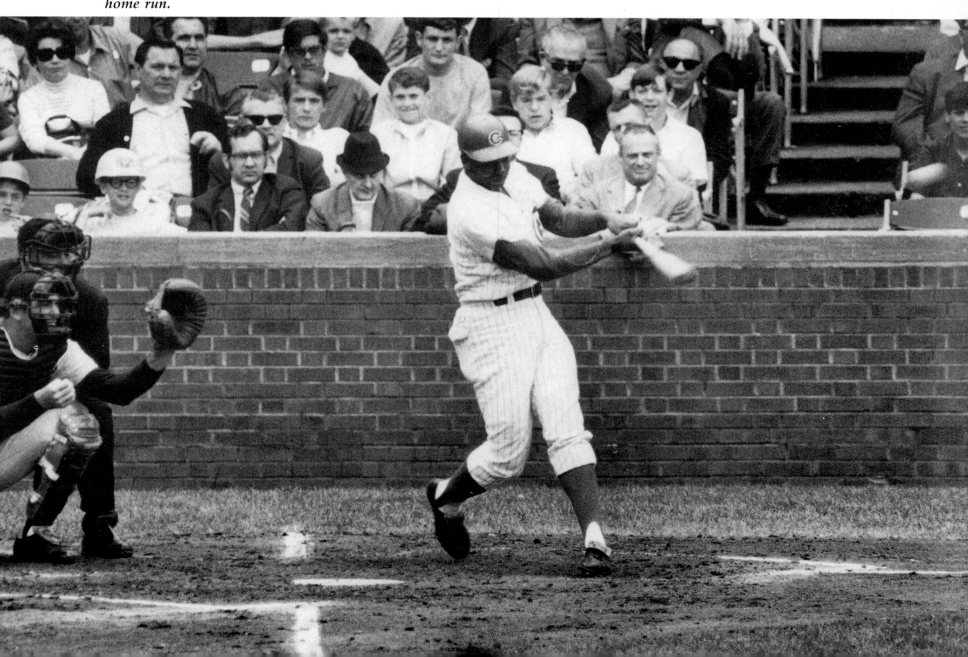

During the 1960s and '70s, Bob Gibson of the Cardinals was one of the game's top pitchers. In 1968, he led the league with a remarkable 1.12 earned run average.

Two other clubs were emerging as powerhouses in the early '70s. They were the flamboyant Oakland A's, who won five straight American League West titles and three world championships under the raucous ownership of Charles 0. Finley, and Cincinnati's Big Red Machine, which won five National League West titles, four pennants and two world championships from 1970–76. Over that stretch, the A's and Reds met just once—in the 1972 World Series. They battled for seven games, six of them decided by one run, as Oakland claimed the first of three straight world championships. Those A's were a wild team, characterized by their outspoken owner. Finley was an innovative character who dressed his team in gaudy gold and green uniforms that were at first derided but remain the team's colors years after he sold the club. He introduced a team mascot— a mule named Charley 0., after the often obstreperous owner. He came up with strange nicknames for his players—Catfish for pitcher Jim Hunter, Blue Moon for pitcher John Odom. He promoted Mustache Day, paying his players $300 for growing them. Reliever Rollie Fingers took that challenge further than the others, cultivating a handsome handlebar version. He got the same $300 as everyone else, though.

One of Finley's ideas was to pump up lagging offenses. He suggested a designated hitter for the pitcher, a sort of perpetual pinch hitter who would bat instead of the pitcher and would not play the field. The American League adopted that revolutionary idea in 1973 but the National League, preferring traditional nine-man baseball, refused to go along. It remains a holdout against the DH—the only league, amateur, minor or major, to reject the idea. By 1973, Hank Aaron's steady attack on pitchers had delivered him into power territory that had been visited only once before—by the great Babe Ruth. Fifteen times, the Braves' slugger hit 30 or more home runs in a season. Seven times, he hit 40 or more and by the end of 1973, he had 713 career homers, one short of Ruth's storied record.

When Oakland beat the Los Angeles Dodgers in the 1974 World Series, it marked the A's third consecutive world championship.

Hank Aaron hits #714 in Cincinnati.

Hank Aaron is congratulated for breaking Babe Ruth's record.

Hank Aaron hits record-breaking home run #715.

Aaron waited through what must have seemed an endless winter and then, on his first swing on Opening Day, 1974, he hit his 714th against Cincinnati's Jack Billingham. Four days later, with the Braves back in Atlanta, he connected for No. 715 against Al Downing of the Los Angeles Dodgers. He would hit 40 more homers before retiring with a record 755.

Henry Aaron of the Atlanta Braves became baseball's all-time home run champion when he connected for his 715th homer on April 8, 1974, to surpass Babe Ruth. Aaron retired with 755 home runs.

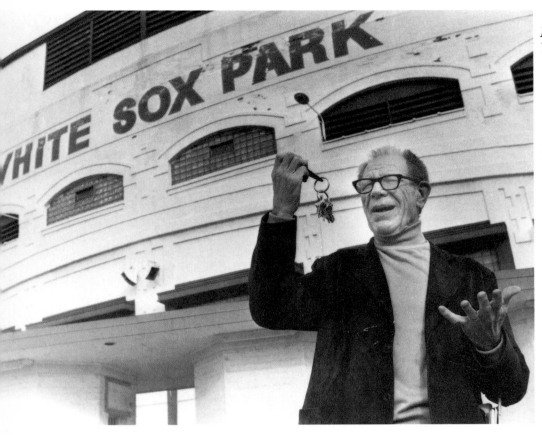

In 1975, Bill Veeck became the owner of the Chicago White Sox.

In 1975, Frank Robinson became the major league's first black manager, with the Cleveland Indians. He also served as the team's designated hitter, and hit a home run in his first at bat.

Oakland's third straight world championship that year ended on a discordant note. Catfish Hunter, the league leader with 25 victories and a 2.49 earned run average, claimed that Finley had broken his contract by refusing to make certain insurance payments. The remedy Hunter asked for was free agency. The issue went to arbitration and, to Finley's consternation, Catfish was set free, permitted to sell himself to the highest bidder. It was the first crack in the reserve clause that tied players to their teams until sold, traded or released. And when the bidding opened, Hunter was astounded at the contracts he was offered. He settled on a five-year, $3 million deal from the New York Yankees. Baseball was suddenly moving into uncharted economic waters. Encouraged by Hunter's bonanza free agent contract following the favorable arbitration decision, the players association decided to press the issue a bit further in 1975. One of the more controversial provisions of the reserve clause permitted teams to renew the contracts of holdout players. The question was whether that renewal could be for more than one season. To test the issue, two pitchers—Andy Messersmith of the Los Angeles Dodgers and Dave McNally, then with the Montreal Expos—went through the entire 1975 season playing under the renewal provision, refusing to sign new deals. At the end of the season, the issue was presented to arbitrator Peter Seitz. Could Messersmith

and McNally be renewed again in 1976 or had their clubs relinquished further hold on the pitchers? Seitz deliberated for several weeks and eventually ruled for the players. They were free agents, the first of scores of players who eventually would walk away from their teams to sign with the highest bidder.

McNally chose to retire from baseball but Messersmith went to the Atlanta Braves after a spirited bidding war. And the uncharted economic waters would turn out to be awfully deep. The end of the 1974 season saw a third no-hitter for Nolan Ryan—he would pitch two more and surge past 5,000 strikeouts in the years to come—and the appointment of Frank Robinson as baseball's first black manager. It had been 27 years since Jackie Robinson became the first black player and the game had changed drastically in that quarter-century or so, with the introduction of domed stadiums and artificial playing surfaces. But until the Cleveland Indians gave Robinson, a future Hall of Famer, a chance, no black had managed a team.

Robinson would be a player-manager and he celebrated his debut with a home run on the opening day of 1975. Ryan pitched his fourth no-hitter and Rod Carew won his fourth straight batting title. But the season belonged to one of the most memorable World Series in history, a brilliant showdown between the Boston Red Sox and Cincinnati Reds.

When Nolan Ryan was with the California Angels, one of his pitches was electronically measured at 100.8 mph, which probably came as no surprise to opposing batters.

Red Sox leftfielder Carl Yastrzemski played 3,308 games, second only to Pete Rose in major league history. He collected 3,419 hits, 452 home runs.

The Red Sox had knocked off Oakland in the playoffs, preventing a possible fourth straight world championship for the A's. The Reds won their division by 20 games and eliminated Pittsburgh in the playoffs. The Series began in Boston and the teams split the first two games, the Red Sox winning the opener 6–0 behind Luis Tiant, the Reds taking Game Two 3–2 on two runs in the top of the ninth. There were six home runs in Game Three with Dwight Evans hitting a two-run shot for Boston in the top of the ninth to force the game into extra innings. Cincinnati won it in the 10th on a bases-loaded single by Joe Morgan after the Red Sox protested to no avail that catcher Carlton Fisk had been interfered with on a bunt play.

Tiant tied the Series at 2–2, winning Game Five 5–4 with a gritty, 163-pitch outing. Then Tony Perez, battling an 0-for-15 Series slump, smashed two home runs giving the Reds a 6–2 victory in Game Five. Now one victory away from the title, the Reds traveled back to Boston. When they got there, it started to rain and it didn't stop for three days. By the time Game Six was played, the two teams were stir crazy. But they put on some show. Fred Lynn, who would sweep both Rookie of the Year and MVP awards, hit a three-run homer in the first inning for the Red Sox. But the Reds clawed back against Tiant, scoring three in the fifth, two in the seventh and another in the eighth for a 6–3 lead. In the bottom of the eighth with two on and two out, Bernie Carbo rescued the Red Sox with an electrifying pinch home run that tied the score. In the bottom of the ninth, Boston loaded the bases with none out and Lynn hit

Carl Yastrzemski and Johnny Bench join the Hall of Fame.

a fly ball to left field. George Foster caught the ball and then uncorked a perfect throw home to double up Denny Doyle and cut the heart out of the rally. Now the game, which was turning into an epic, moved into extra innings. In the 11th, Dwight Evans made a leaping one-handed catch in front of the right field bleachers, robbing Joe Morgan of an apparent home run. The catch

was so improbable that Evans had no trouble doubling up Ken Griffey, who was all the way to third when he grabbed the ball. The teams moved into the 12th inning and Carlton Fisk, leading off for Boston, sent Pat Darcy's second pitch down the left field line. With Fisk waving furiously, trying to guide the ball fair, it hit high off the foul pole for the game-winning home run.

Reds' catcher Johnny Bench homered in the third game of the 1975 World Series against Boston. He won two

National League Most Valuable Player awards and two home run titles.

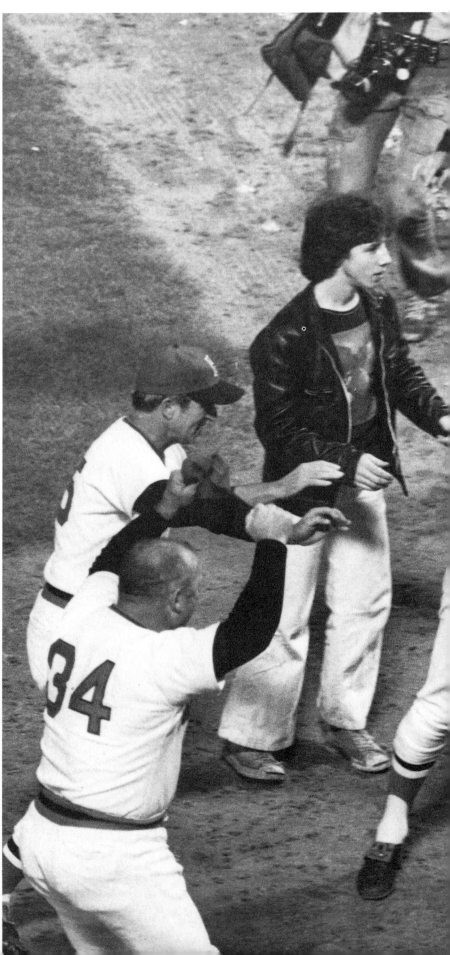

Red Sox catcher Carlton Fisk hit a dramatic 12th-inning home run to give Boston the sixth game of the 1975 World Series against Cincinnati.

The next night in the winner-take-all seventh game, Boston struck first, scoring three runs in the bottom of the third inning. Tony Perez got two of them back with a home run in the sixth and then tied it in the seventh on a single by Pete Rose. In the ninth, Griffey led off with a walk and advanced to third on a sacrifice and an infield out. That brought up Rose with Joe Morgan on deck. As they came out of the dugout, Rose turned to his teammate and said, "If I don't do it, you will."

He was right. Rose walked and Morgan singled to center scoring the deciding run of one of baseball's greatest World Series.

A host of players used the Messersmith-McNally precedent to play out their contractual obligations in 1976 and the Reds' four-game sweep of the Yankees—back in the World Series after a dozen years—was overshadowed by the beckoning break-the-bank auction for top free agents.

The Series was a brilliant showdown between the rival catchers. Thurman Munson of New York batted.529 and Johnny Bench of the Reds hit.533 as Cincinnati became the first National League team since 1922 to win two straight world championships. Perhaps the biggest jewel in the free agent market after the 1976 season was outfielder Reggie Jackson. He had been a key part of Oakland's three straight world championships but often clashed with Charles 0. Finley, as did so many of the A's. Once when Jackson was asked how he would do in another setting, he smiled broadly. "If I played in New York," he said, "they'd name a candy bar for me."

He would and they did.

Reggie Jackson hit a home run for the Oakland A's in the 1975 American League Championship Series against Boston. Jackson's postseason heroics earned him the nickname Mr. October.

The Series was a brilliant showdown between the rival catchers. Thurman Munson of New York batted .529 and Johnny Bench of the Reds hit .533 as Cincinnati became the first National League team since 1922 to win two straight world championships.

Perhaps the biggest jewel in the free agent market after the 1976 season was outfielder Reggie Jackson. He had been a key part of Oakland's three straight world championships but often clashed with Charles 0. Finley, as did so many of the A's. Once when Jackson was asked how he would do in another setting, he smiled broadly. "If I played in New York," he said, "they'd name a candy bar for me."

He would and they did.

Reggie Jackson blasts home run #3 during final game of '77 Series.

Reggie Jackson missed this pitch, but connected on enough to collect 593 home runs, placing him sixth on the all-time list.

Rejecting what was described as "a king's ransom," from Montreal, Jackson signed with the Yankees, joining Catfish Hunter as New York's second $3 million man. To say he did not fit into the Yankee chemistry would be an understatement. There were public clashes with Munson and fiery manager Billy Martin, who nearly came to blows with Jackson in full view of network television cameras in Fenway Park.

Somehow, they learned to live together and carried the Yankees to still another pennant. Then, in the World Series, Jackson wrote a little history, ripping five home runs, the last three in Game Six as New York defeated Los Angeles for the world championship. Only Babe Ruth had ever hit three homers in a single Series game and no man had ever hit five in one Series. But Jackson, who was called Mr. October for his late-season heroics, flourished in the soap opera setting of the Yankee clubhouse, enjoying every moment in the spotlight.

And the next spring, a candy company marketed the first Reggie Bars.

The Yankees' Reggie Jackson was the picture of consistency as he hit three home runs to help defeat the Los Angeles Dodgers in the final game of the 1977 World Series.

Willie Stargell was elected to the Hall of Fame in his first year of eligibility.

In 1978, the turmoil of the Yankees spilled over. Martin's feuds with Jackson and owner George Steinbrenner became a public embarrassment and his first term as manager ended in mid-season. He would return, however, many times.

The Yankees fell 14 games behind Boston but then staged a stirring recovery, catching the Red Sox in September and forcing a one-game playoff for the division title. A stunning three-run homer by Bucky Dent brought New York from behind and gave the Yankees the division. For the third straight year, New York eliminated Kansas City in the playoffs and the Yankees went on to beat Los Angeles again in six games, winning the last four after dropping the first two.

As the decade of the '70s ended, there were labor clouds on the horizon. Baseball had adopted a get-tough attitude with the umpires union, going through seven weeks of the 1979 season with substitute officials as the regular umps walked picket lines. It was widely believed to be a signal to the players that the owners would have a tough negotiating stance when the basic agreement expired.

The last world championship of the decade went to Pittsburgh, with the Pirates climbing out of a 3–1 hole to overtake Baltimore in a World Series that was reminiscent of the 1971 matchup when the Orioles won the first two games only to lose to Pittsburgh in seven. The hero was the old man of the team, first baseman Willie Stargell, who tagged a two-run homer in the sixth inning of the final game to give the Pirates the lead for good. It was Stargell who had pulled the team together during the season, borrowing the slogan "We Are Family" from a popular rock group and riding it to the world championship.

Lou Brock steals second.

Slugger Willie Stargell had some great years for the
Pittsburgh Pirates. He hit 475 lifetime home runs and
led the league in homers twice.

On August 29, 1977, Lou Brock stole his 893rd base, breaking the record held by Ty Cobb. Brock finished his career with 938 steals.

NINTH INNING

9

TRIUMPH AND TRAGEDY 1980–1989

Ted Williams once tried to explain why the fine art of hitting, which seemed to come so easily to him, was so complicated for others. "They give you a round ball and a round bat, "Williams said dryly, "and then they tell you to hit it squarely." Fail seven times in 10 tries at that tricky assignment and you're a star. Fail six times out of 10—as Williams did in 1941 when he was base-ball's last .400 hitter—and you're in a special class, a baseball fraternity with precious few members, a club that has admitted no one in nearly half a century. In 1980, George Brett sought admission to the .400 club and came closer to getting in than anybody had since Williams batted .406 in that special summer of '41. Brett, the third baseman of the Kansas City Royals, was trou-bled by nagging foot injuries all season that limited him to 117 games. But when he was in the lineup, he was like a hitting machine with his stroke locked in, nail-ing everything pitchers could offer. Brett went to bat 449 times that season, collecting 175 hits for a sizzling .390 pace.

How close did he come to .400?

George Brett.

To reach that average, he would have needed just five more hits in the same number of at-bats.

Five hits in five months. That's how close George Brett came to batting .400.

Before the 1980 season began, Nolan Ryan signed a free agent contract with Houston that broke new sal-ary barriers. Ryan would be paid $1 million a year in a sport where for decades no player had ever made more than $100,000. Ryan earned his status with a breathtaking fastball that produced four no-hitters in the mid-'70s with California and would generate a fifth with the Astros in 1981.

Ryan's Astros went into the final weekend of the 1980 season with a three-game lead over Los Angeles and three games remaining, all of them with the Dodgers. LA swept the series, forcing a one-game divisional playoff but lost the final showdown, sending the As-tros into the pennant playoff against Philadelphia. The series went the five-game limit with four of them stretching into extra innings.

Royals third baseman George Brett is best known for his skills with the bat. He has won two batting league titles, hitting a lofty .390 in 1980.

Finally, the Phillies captured the flag, their first pennant in 30 years and only the third in franchise history. Waiting for the Phils were Brett's Royals. Kansas City had lost three straight playoffs to the New York Yankees but, given a fourth chance, the Royals prevailed in a three-game sweep that was punctuated by Brett's three-run homer against relief ace Goose Gossage that clinched the flag.

The World Series went six games with the Phillies prevailing, nailing down the world championship in most dramatic fashion. When Kansas City loaded the bases in the ninth inning of the final game, reliever Tug McGraw got Frank White to hit a lazy foul pop near the Philadelphia dugout. Sure-handed catcher Bob Boone got a late start on the ball but was there in time to make the catch. It plopped into his glove—and then plopped right out. As Phillies fans gasped, first baseman Pete Rose, who had come over to converge on the ball with Boone, snatched it out of the air, saving the out. It was typical Rose, hustling all the time, taking nothing for granted, asking no quarter and giving none. McGraw then struck out Willie Wilson to finish off the Royals. At the end of that season, Rose had 3,557 career hits—634 away from Ty Cobb's record. The countdown had begun, much as it had for Hank Aaron when he was chasing the ghost of Babe Ruth's home run record. Rose's first target would be Stan Musial's National League hit record, just 73 hits away. Then, a strange thing happened. They stopped playing baseball games.

A couple of baseball's superstars were involved in this play, as Cincinnati's Pete Rose reaches third base safely despite the efforts of the Phillies' Mike Schmidt.

The labor powder keg that baseball had been sitting on so precariously exploded in the summer of 1981 with a 50-day strike that halted the season. At issue was management's demand for replacement players for those lost by their clubs to free agency. The union saw that as a tactic to restrict free agency and shut down the game—and Rose's pursuit of Musial and Cobb—for close to two months in the middle of the season. When the strike was settled and play resumed, the owners adopted a split-season plan, establishing a second layer of playoffs, to cope with the truncated season. The solution pleased just about no one, least of all the Cincinnati Reds, who had baseball's best record for the year but, because they did not finish first in either half of the suddenly-divided season, were left on the outside of the playoffs. The Reds howled mightily over that misdemeanor and lined up solidly in the corner of a slowly-developing faction of owners who opposed the administration of commissioner Bowie Kuhn. Eventually, there would be enough of them to bring Kuhn down. Rose led the majors with 140 hits in the shortened season and was at 3,697—less than 500 hits away from Cobb. There was a time when that would have been less than three years work for him, when he regularly produced 200-hit seasons. Now, though, Rose was 40 years old. The hits were becoming harder to come by and there seemed some question whether he would make it. They were exacerbated in 1982, when his production dwindled to a .271 batting average and 172 hits and then 1983 when, as the Phillies won still another pennant, Rose managed just 121 hits and a .245 batting average. His contract in Philadelphia was up. He was 42 now, commanding a

Mike Schmidt hits his 536th home run.

Pete Rose was Cincinnatti's player-manager when he scored this 10th-inning winning run in a game against the San Francisco Giants.

high salary with little left as a player, and still 201 hits away from Cobb. Rose searched for a club that would be willing to hire him for the last lap of his marathon run and settled in Montreal. It was only a short stay, though, because before season's end, he was back where he had started in Cincinnati, doubling as player-manager of the Reds. He finished 1984 with 107 hits, still 94 short. It would take him five months to reach the target. Finally, on September 11, 1985, Rose achieved his goal, dropping a hump-back line drive into left field at Cincinnati's Riverfront Stadium against Eric Show of the San Diego Padres for the 4,192nd hit of his career. As he stood at first base, embraced by his son and his teammates, tears welled in Rose's eyes. Within a few years, however, others would cry for him.

The fascination with Rose's pursuit of Cobb was interrupted during the summer of 1983 by the infamous

Pete Rose strokes single to break Ty Cobb's hit mark.

A head-first view of first base and dirty uniform were familiar sights to Pete Rose throughout his long and productive career.

Philadelphia Phillies third baseman Mike Schmidt hit a 10th inning home run that beat the Cubs in a remarkable 23–22 game in 1979.

The Phillies' Mike Schmidt was a superb glove man as well as a great slugger. He is seventh on the all-time home run list with 548 and led the National League in homers eight times.

In September 1985, the Reds' Pete Rose collected his 4,192nd base hit to surpass Ty Cobb and make Rose baseball's all-time leading hit-maker. Rose retired with a record 4,256 hits.

Nolan Ryan.

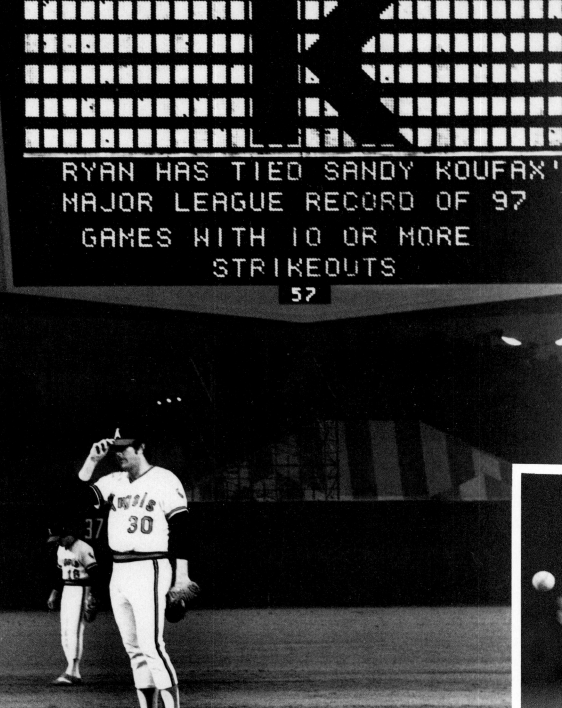

Hard-throwing Nolan Ryan owns plenty of strikeout records, including most career strikeouts—a phenomenal 5,076 through the 1989 season.

Nolan Ryan got his 200th career win in 1982 in the uniform of the Houston Astros.

pine tar affair that centered around George Brett and the New York Yankees. Brett had tagged Yankee relief ace Goose Gossage for a monstrous three-run homer that decided the 1980 pennant playoffs. Now three years later, the same two confronted each other in an August game at Yankee Stadium. Gossage was trying to nail down a 4–3 New York victory when Brett, batting with a runner on first and two out in the ninth inning, caught another of Goose's fast balls and sent it into the right field seats for a dramatic home run that put Kansas City ahead. As Brett circled the bases, Billy Martin, serving the third of his five stints as manager of the Yankees, strolled up to home plate and asked the umpires to examine Brett's bat. Martin's argument was that Brett had pine tar past the 18-inch limit, making the bat and consequently the home run illegal. Umpire Joe Brinkman's crew listened to Martin's reasoned contention and agreed with him. When home plate umpire Tim McClelland signalled the out—which would have ended the game with the Yankees winning 4–3—Brett came racing out of the dugout, so angry it seemed that he might get into a physical confrontation with the umpires. He was eventually restrained and the Royals protested the call, saying that it was not in the spirit of the rule. Pine tar helps the grip. It does not contribute to distance. American League president Lee MacPhail later agreed with the Royals contention and ordered the balance of the game—four outs with Kansas City leading 5–4—played three weeks later. Martin never accepted the interpretation, although MacPhail's ruling stood.

The pine tar affair was MacPhail's last hurrah as American League president. Baseball's executive suite began undergoing substantial changes in 1984. After a search that stretched some 15 months, the owners selected businessman Peter Ueberroth to succeed Bowie Kuhn as commissioner. The same year, MacPhail left the American League office to Dr. Bobby Brown, a former major league third baseman who had become a prominent cardiologist. And three years later, A. Bartlett Giamatti would succeed Chub Feeney as National League president and then Ueberroth as commissioner. Ueberroth came to baseball with impressive credentials. By selling corporate sponsorships—a wrinkle that once would have been dismissed summarily by amateur sports officials—he had turned the perennially debt-ridden Summer Olympics into a huge money-maker in 1984. He would do the same thing for baseball, presiding over a period of unparalleled growth for the game, with annual attendances pushing past 50 million and a number of teams drawing over 3 million in a season during his administration. Ueberroth succeeded in extinguishing a number of brush fires during his term in office, and benefited from some of baseball's most exciting postseason moments. When he arrived in the commissioner's office, he found the umpires on strike for the start of the 1984 playoffs. Within a week, he had them back on the job for the World Series. A year later, when the players went on strike again, his work behind the scenes helped forge a settlement after just two days. Those two labor affairs were in sharp contrast to the seven-week strikes baseball had endured from the umpires in 1979 and the players in 1981.

Early on in his administration, Ueberroth surveyed the baseball landscape and found no sign of two of the game's greatest recent stars—Mickey Mantle and Willie Mays. Both had taken jobs with gambling casinos, serving as hosts and glad-handers for the high rollers. Bowie Kuhn ruled that as long as they were linked with the casino community, they could not participate in baseball, even as token spring training coaches. Kuhn banned both from baseball, a less-than-popular move that he believed necessary for the integrity of the game. Ueberroth examined the situation, decided that Mays and Mantle were not involved in any activity that could pose a problem for the game and set aside Kuhn's ruling, welcoming the Hall of Famers back in baseball's good graces. The decision was a public relations coup for the commissioner, who always excelled in that arena.

There was, for example, the issue of drugs. Substance

abuse became a widespread problem during the early part of the decade and the matter came to a head in 1985 when some of the game's premier players were served with subpoenas to testify before a federal grand jury at drug trials in Pittsburgh. The following spring, Ueberroth moved against 21 players, handing down suspensions that were conditional. The players were permitted to buy their way back into baseball's good graces by paying substantial fines and agreeing to do community service. Again, it was a public relations bonanza for Ueberroth, who had handed down punishment and yet not deprived teams or fans of the players.

In the early part of the decade, salaries continued to grow and outfielder George Foster pushed the limit past $2 million a year. Free agency and salary arbitration was turning the players into capitalists and it seemed there would be no limit. Then, suddenly, the bottom fell out of the market. Teams with histories of wide open wallets turned the other way when free agents came along. Jack Morris, who would win more games than any other pitcher during the '80s, went on a shopping tour looking for a new team and was turned away at every stop. Nobody needed Morris' consistent 20-win potential. Sorry, they told him.

The players association smelled a rat and charged the owners with collusion. Management said it was no such thing, just an attack of good judgment. An arbitrator agreed with the union, though, and tagged management with heavy penalties for violating the basic agreement that prohibited such behavior.

Baseball commissioner Peter Ueberroth unveiled the logo for the 1986 All-Star Game, played at Houston's Astrodome.

Meanwhile, baseball was blessed with two terrific playoff and World Series shows in 1985 and 1986. First, in '85, Dick Howser's Kansas City Royals turned in two spectacular comebacks in the playoffs and World Series. Only rarely had teams been able to recover from 3–1 deficits in best-of-seven series because that kind of hole leaves no margin for mistakes. The 1985 Royals did it not once, but twice.

Trailing Toronto in the playoffs, the Royals swept the last three games to advance to the World Series. The Blue Jays had been victimized by a change in the format, extending the championship series from best-of-5 to best-of-7 which left room for the Royals to recover.

In the World Series, Kansas City lost the first two games at home to St. Louis and were trailing the Cardinals 3–1. But they weren't being blown away. The Cardinals' pattycake attack had won 3–1, 3–2 and 3–0, leaving St. Louis vulnerable in every game. The Royals won Game Five in St. Louis, sending the Series back to Kansas City. It looked like it was all over in Game Six with the Royals trailing 1–0 and down to their last three outs. Pinch hitter Jorge Orta opened the inning with a grounder to first. Reliever Todd Worrell was a step slow covering the base and Orta was called safe by umpire Don Denkinger. Television replays showed that Jack Clark's toss to Worrell had beaten Orta to the bag but the call gave the Royals their opening.

After Clark missed Steve Balboni's foul pop, the opening became a chasm. Balboni singled and, after Orta was forced at third on an attempted sacrifice, a passed ball allowed the runners to advance. Then, pinch hitter Dane Iorg singled, chasing home the tying and winning runs.

The next night, the Cardinals, who had been two outs away from the world championship, simply came apart at the seams. St. Louis was routed 11–0 as the Royals, who had spent all of October living on the edge, enjoyed a cakewalk to the championship.

In 1986, California had Boston at a 3–1 disadvantage in the American League playoffs. The Angels, playing at home, led by three runs in the ninth inning of Game Five and were ready to rush the field and celebrate their first division championship. Then it all collapsed. Home runs by Don Baylor and Dave Henderson fueled a furious Red Sox comeback. Boston won that game and the next two to advance to the World Series. There, they found the New York Mets, who arrived there in similarly unusual fashion.

The Mets had run away with the NL East race, winning 108 games and finishing 21 games in front. In the playoff, they faced a strong Houston club, winners by 10 in the West. The Astros were carried by Mike Scott, master of the split-fingered fast ball, whose no-hitter had clinched the division for Houston. Scott at that stage bordered on the unhittable, certainly for the Mets, who lost twice to him in the first five games of the playoff. For Game Six, the Mets played with a sense of urgency, knowing if they lost and went to a Game Seven they would face Scott again. They were at a psychological disadvantage against him and they knew it. Trailing 3–0 in the ninth inning, and with Scott ominously flipping a ball in the Houston dugout, the Mets were desperate. They rallied against Bob Knepper, scoring three times to tie the game. In the 14th inning, they took the lead, only to have Billy Hatcher tie it for Houston with a home run in the bottom of the

New York Mets celebrate victory over Red Sox.

inning. In the 16th, New York scored three times, seeming to finish off the Astros. But once again Houston rallied, this time for two runs. The Astros had the tying and winning runs on base when the final out was recorded, ending baseball's most monumental playoffs since the Bobby Thomson home run in 1951.

In the World Series, the Mets got into the same kind of trouble Kansas City had the year before, losing the first two games at home. New York won two of three in Boston but still trailed three games to two going into Game Six. When the Red Sox broke a 10th inning tie with two runs—the first on another home run by Dave Henderson—it seemed Boston would win its first World Series since 1918. The Mets had two out and nobody on in the bottom of the 10th when Gary Carter lined a stay-alive single to center field. Kevin Mitchell and Ray Knight followed with hits, narrowing the Red Sox lead to a single run. Then a wild pitch by reliever Bob Stanley scored Mitchell with the tying run. When Mookie Wilson's trickler down the first base line went through sore-ankled Bill Buckner's legs, Knight raced home with the run that gave the Mets a most improbable victory. It was almost anticlimactic when New York wiped out another deficit in Game Seven to win the World Series.

Ueberroth dedicated the 1987 baseball season to the 40th anniversary of Jackie Robinson's debut in the major leagues which opened baseball to black players. On opening night, however, Dodger General Manager Al Campanis was interviewed on a national television program to discuss Robinson and the black issue. Campanis, who had played shortstop alongside Robinson in the minor leagues, was asked about the progress of blacks beyond player status and blundered terribly, saying they "may not have some of the necessities to be, let's say, a field manager or a general manager."

Peter Ueberroth.

MVP Ray Knight celebrates with champagne.

It was an insensitive remark by a man who, ironically, had been at the forefront of introducing Latin and
other minority players into the Dodger system. Campanis was dismissed, but his remark sparked a push
for affirmative action in baseball, a commitment to hir-
ing minorities for off-field jobs.

That fall, St. Louis returned to the World Series for
the third time in the decade, this time against Minnesota. Never had the home field advantage been so
pronounced. The Twins, playing in their domed stadium, won the first two games at home, lost the next three
in St. Louis and swept the final two at home, again,
to claim the title. It was the first time in history that
the home team had won every game in the Series.

*Bowie Kuhn served as a commissioner of baseball for
15 years.*

George Brett makes a diving grab.

Through the 1989 season, Rickey Henderson had accumulated 871 stolen bases to put him third on the all-time list behind Lou Brock (938) and Ty Cobb (892).

Baseball moved into an era of parity following the two straight Los Angeles Dodger–New York Yankee World Series of 1977–1978. No team would repeat pennant winners until 1989 when the Oakland A's took their second straight American League flag. The A's rode the 40 home run and 40 stolen base season of Jose Canseco to the 1988 title. It was the first time in history that a player had combined those two diverse skills of power and speed to reach those plateaus.

That same summer, pitcher Orel Hershiser of the Los Angeles Dodgers got locked into a zone rarely visited by a pitcher. Starting with the sixth inning of an August 30 game at Montreal, Hershiser stopped surrendering runs. There were six consecutive shutouts, the last one 10 innings, stretching his streak to a record 59 innings, breaking the mark set 20 years before by Don Drysdale.

The World Series between the Dodgers and A's turned in the first game. With LA slugger Kirk Gibson sidelined by hamstring and knee injuries, the Dodgers trailed 4–3 in the ninth inning against Oakland relief ace Dennis Eckersley. With a runner on first and two out, Gibson came limping out of the Dodger dugout to pinch hit. Eckersley put him in a two-strike hole as Gibson swung feebly. Then, with the A's one strike away from victory, Gibson took one more swing and sent a drive into the right field seats, a two-run homer that turned the game and the Series. The A's never recovered, losing to LA in five games.

Dodger pitcher Orel Hershisher pitched his team to playoff and World Series victories in 1988.

Dodger pitcher Orel Hershiser stunned the Oakland A's by beating them in five games in the 1988 World Series. Catcher Rick Dempsey lifted pitcher Hershiser in celebration of the victory.

Kirk Gibson celebrates home run with teammates and manager, Tom Lasorda.

The following spring, Bart Giamatti was preparing to succeed Peter Ueberroth, who decided that one term as commissioner was enough for him. Ueberroth was turning over a flourishing industry, a sport enjoying record attendances. There was, however, one small problem. There was the matter of Pete Rose.

The commissioner's office had reports that Rose, now retired as a player but still managing the Reds, was deeply involved with gamblers and bookmakers and might even be betting on baseball. Rose was summoned from spring training to meet with the incoming and out-going commissioners. Baseball launched an investigation and Rose fought the game at every turn, winning small victories in a local court, losing larger issues in federal court. Finally, with evidence against him mounting, Rose accepted Giamatti's sentence—a lifetime ban from baseball. The issue dominated the five-month commissionership of the former Yale president. Eight days after banning Rose, Giamatti died of a massive heart attack at his vacation home in Martha's Vineyard, Massachusetts.

The loss of Giamatti was an enormous shock for base-ball. Less than two months later, the game was faced with another jolt—this one literal. As Oakland and San Francisco were preparing for the third game of the 1989 World Series, a huge earthquake shook Northern California. The ground rumbled, the upper deck at Candlestick Park trembled, the light towers swayed. The quake caused huge devastation throughout the Bay Area and Fay Vincent, the new commissioner of base-ball, acted sensitively in the midst of the crisis, delaying the Series for 10 days until the community could recover.

Vincent had handled his first crisis with compassion and understanding and an insight that would have pleased Giamatti. The scholar who served as commissioner for just five months had a lifelong love affair for the game, a passion for its place in the history of the country.

Asked to describe the sport he loved so much, Giamatti once offered this thought.

"Baseball is its own long poem," he said, "its own endless epic."

The epic poem continues.

Pete Rose signals thumbs-up to fans while controversy swirls around him.

Bart Giamatti at news conference announcing his decision on Pete Rose.

EXTRA INNINGS

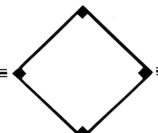

GLORY AND UNCERTAINTY

If Reggie Jackson was baseball's exclamation mark for the '70s and Nolan Ryan was the centerpiece of the '80s, then slugger Barry Bonds and pitcher Greg Maddux have been the signature players for the early '90s.

And those signatures could be at the bottom of some very expensive free agent contracts.

Bonds won three Most Valuable Player awards in the first four years of the decade, the first two with Pittsburgh in 1990 and 1992, and the third one with San Francisco in 1993. He moved to the Giants after signing a record $43.75 million free agent contract and proved to be worth every penny of the deal, nearly carrying his new club to the National League West title. Bonds batted .336 and led the league with 46 home runs and 123 runs batted in.

Maddux, like Bonds a hot commodity on the free agent market after winning 20 games and the Cy Young Award for the lowly Chicago Cubs in 1992, signed a $28 million deal with the Atlanta Braves and merely repeated his production in the new setting. He again won 20 games, led the league with a 2.36 earned run average, and again won the Cy Young Award, becoming the first National League pitcher to repeat that feat since Sandy Koufax. Over six seasons beginning in 1988, Maddux led all NL pitchers in wins (107), starts (212) and complete games (48).

Despite their individual accomplishments, Bonds and Maddux were unable to carry their teams to postseason success. In fact, both experienced serious disappointments in October. Bonds struggled through three dreadful playoffs with Pittsburgh, which came oh-so-close to the World Series before falling short. And Maddux lost the deciding game for the Braves after Atlanta had posted the best record in baseball with 104 victories—one more

Los Angeles Dodgers pitcher Fernando Valenzuela on his way to the first no-hitter of his career, a 6-0 game over the St. Louis Cardinals in June 1990.

than Bonds' Giants managed.

Both Bonds and Maddux signed their fat contracts after rejecting feverish overtures by the New York Yankees. It was in the free agent market that Yankee owner George Steinbrenner had flourished before and after sitting out a 2 1/2 - year suspension for his association with a gambler. Steinbrenner seemed determined to celebrate his return to baseball with a big money signing. Bonds and Maddux wouldn't bite but Steinbrenner found other customers like Wade Boggs and Jimmy Key, who both helped the Yankees put on a spirited run at the Al East title and make it a satisfying season for the Boss.

Steinbrenner's latest problems with baseball began when he admitted paying off a gambler to dig up dirt on Dave Winfield. Once welcomed as one of the Yankee owner's free agent jewels, Winfield's relations with the Boss had soured considerably, so much that Steinbrenner wound up in hot water for pursuing his attack on the outfielder. Cincinnati owner Marge Schott also sat out a season for intemperate remarks, leaving baseball on the same day Steinbrenner returned from his exile.

Ironically, in the same year that Steinbrenner was restored to baseball's good graces, Winfield swatted his 3,000th career hit, bringing home the winning run in the World Series for the Toronto Blue Jays in the process.

Those 1992 Toronto champions underwent a drastic overhaul with a dozen players, including Winfield, either traded or signed with other teams. It hardly disturbed the production of the club. General manager Pat Gillick imported quality replacements and the Jays repeated as world champions, defeating Philadelphia in six games when Joe Carter, one of the 1992 Jays who stuck around for '93, hit a home run in the bottom of the ninth inning of the decisive game. It was just the second time in baseball history that a home run ended the World Series, joining Bill Mazeroski's dramatic blow in Game Seven of the 1960 Series. Carter's homer made Toronto the first team to repeat a world championship since the 1977-78 New York Yankees.

Philadelphia's appearance in the World Series was an achievement in and of itself. The Phillies had finished in last place the year before, and ordinarily their worst-to-first reversal would have been a stunner. The only thing was, two years before, Minnesota and Atlanta pulled off the same trick and met in the 1991 World Series.

The decade began with the punctuation on pitching. In 1990, there were a record nine no-hitters, four of them in the month of June. Two of those came on the same night, June 29, when Oakland's Dave Stewart no-hit Toronto and, a couple of hours later, Fernando Valenzuela of the Dodgers did the same thing to St. Louis. It marked the only time in this century that two complete game no-hitters occurred on the same date.

Naturally, Nolan Ryan pitched one of 1990's no-hitters, the sixth of this remarkable career. He also won his 300th game and then, a year later, at age 44, he pitched no-hitter number 7. It should be noted that Ryan still had seven no-hitters after a statistical committee, deputized by commissioner Fay Vincent, combed through the record book to tighten the definition of no-hitters and purged 50 of them. Among the casualties were perfect games by Harvey Haddix, who retired 36 straight batters before giving up a hit, and Ernie Shore, who came in after the first batter reached base and then retired 26 in a row after the runner was thrown out trying to steal. Also eliminated was the controversial asterisk—which never really appeared in the record book anyway—that tainted Roger Maris' 61 home runs because they occurred in a 162-game season instead of the 154 in which Babe Ruth hit his 60.

Maris' accomplishment came in 1961, an expansion season, and baseball was ready for more of the same in 1993 when the National League added new franchises in Florida and Colorado for a fee of $95 million each. And although there were some remarkable hitting performances as a result of thinned-out pitching staffs—a bizarre 15-14 game in the World Series was the most glaring example — the most noteworthy results of expansion were that neither new team finished in last place. That dubious distinction went to the New York Mets in the NL East and the San Diego Padres in the West.

Both batting champions, John Olerud of Toronto and Andres Galarraga of Colorado, made runs at .400, although both were well short of the target. Olerud finished at .363 and Galarraga at .370. Olerud, though, led a 1-2-3 finish for Toronto in the batting race with Blue Jays Paul Molitor (.332) and Roberto Alomar (.326) behind him. It was the first time in this century that teammates held down the top three spots in the batting race.

Juan Gonzalez of Texas and San Franciscos' Bonds each hit 46 home runs and 22 players had at least

Ricky Henderson celebrates after setting the all-time stolen base record.

Joe Carter celebrates as he runs the bases after hitting the 1993 World Series-winning three-run homer in the ninth!

30. Included in that group was Ken Giffey Jr., of Seattle, who tied a record with home runs in eight consecutive games. Twenty-five players drove in 100 runs or more and one previously obscure player, Mark Whiten of the St. Louis Cardinals, produced what is arguably the single greatest day of offense in baseball history.

Whiten hit four home runs in one game, becoming the 12th player in history to do that. None of the other 11, however, drove in a dozen runs in one game, which Whiten also accomplished. Hence, the combination produced the greatest one-day rampage ever enjoyed by a batter.

When it comes to offense though, few players made the kind of splash in the '90s that Cecil Fielder of Detroit did. A fringe player in parts of four seasons with Toronto, Fielder took a year off to play in Japan and then returned to the majors with a vengeance. Signed by Detroit, he exploded on the scene with 51 home runs in 1990, the first major leaguer to reach the 50-mark since George Foster in 1977 and the first American Leaguer to do it since Maris and Mickey Mantle in 1961. Fielder drove in 132 runs that season, 133 the next year and then 124 the year after that, becoming the first player since Babe Ruth to lead the majors in RBIs three straight years. Somehow, though, he never managed to win a MVP award despite those numbers.

As dominant as Fielder was at bat in the AL, Boston's Roger Clemens was his match on the mound. Clemens won three straight ERA awards and ran his string of 200-strikeout seasons to seven in a row, tying Hall of Famers Rube Waddell and Walter Johnson. He also won his third Cy Young Award before struggling through a difficult 1993 season.

Among those who beat Fielder out of the MVP award were Rickey Henderson, who hit .325 in 1990 with 28 home runs and stole 65 bases to move within three steals of Lou Brock's all-time record. Henderson matched the mark a year later, but had to share the spotlight that day with Ryan's seventh no-hitter.

There were other important milestones in the early '90s, including the 3,000th hit for George Brett and Robin Yount, both achieved in September, 1992. A year later, Brett (3,154 hits, 317 home runs, 1,595 RBIs) and Ryan (324 wins, 5,714 strikeouts) left baseball altogether along with Carlton Fisk, who caught more games (2,226) than any in history. All three would seem to have a date in the Hall of Fame before the end of the century.

The decade of the '90s began with a shocking World Series. With Pete Rose banned from baseball and in prison for tax evasion, Cincinnati's nightmare was over and the Reds responded brilliantly under expatriate Yankee manager Lou Piniella. The Reds became the first NL team to lead the league for all 162 games. They eliminated Bonds and Pittsburgh in the playoffs and advanced to the Series against Oakland. This was the same A's team that had swept San Francisco in the 1989 Earthquake Series, equipped with a pitching staff headed by 27-game winner Bob Welch and Dave Stewart, who was coming off his straight 20 win season. They were backed by stopper Dennis Eckersley and an offense headed by Henderson and Jose Canseco, the first player to combine 40 steals and 40 homers in the same season.

Oakland was heavily favored but the A's never won a game. Pitcher Jose Rijo, traded by Oakland to the Reds, came back to haunt the A's, beating them twice and being named MVP in Cincinnati's stunning Series sweep.

If Oakland was the cream of the American League West in 1990, then Minnesota was the crust. The Twins finished dead last, well-removed from the playoffs in a season distinguished by the unique achievement of becoming the only team in history to record two triple plays in a single game. A year later, though, the Twins experienced the ultimate reversal of fortune and found themselves division champions.

Minnesota's accomplishment was impressive but no more so than that of the Atlanta Braves, who pulled the same last-to-first trick. No team had ever gone bottom to top in one year and in this year, two did it. The Twins eliminated Toronto in five games and the Braves sent Pittsburgh home in seven, winning the last two on the road on shutouts by Steve Avery and John Smoltz.

The Twins and Braves then staged a titanic World Series that was the closest of all time. Three of the games went to extra innings and four were decided on the last swing. The exclamation point came in Game Seven. Starter Jack Morris for the Twins and Smoltz for the Braves pitched brilliantly and were locked in a scoreless duel after seven innings. Both teams loaded the bases but failed to score in the eighth. Finally, in the 10th, with both teams emotionally exhausted, Minnesota pushed over the winning run on a pinch single by Gene Larkin. When it was over, players on both teams embraced, secure in the knowledge that they had completed one of the greatest World Series ever played.

A year later, Pittsburgh won its third straight NL East title and again found Atlanta waiting in the playoffs. The Pirates and Braves had staged a thrilling show-down in 1991 and this time, there was more of a sense of urgency for Pittsburgh. Bobby Bonilla had already left for a free agent contract with the Mets. Bonds, coming off another MVP season, was certain to follow and so was Doug Drabek, the anchor of the Pirate pitching staff. With limited resources, the Pirates knew they could not afford the contracts their stars would be offered elsewhere.

Again, the teams dueled to a decisive seventh game. Drabek, reaching into a nearly empty pitching reservoir, carried a 2-0 lead into the bottom of the ninth inning. The Pirates were three outs away from the World Series. They only got two of them.

In a thrilling rally, Atlanta came from behind. The Braves were still down 2-1 with runners on second and third when Francisco Cabrera singled to left, scoring the tying run. Then, around third came Sid Bream, running on surgically repaired knees, every step seeming to take an eternity. His desperate slide barely beat the throw by Bonds. For the first time in history, a team one out away from elimination had rallied to win a post season series on a single swing.

The throw that came oh-so-close to saving the Pirates' season turned out to be Bond's last play for Pittsburgh. He departed soon after that for San Francisco, which wasn't even supposed to have a team. The Giants had been sold to interests in Tampa, Florida and were expected to move. But NL owners blocked the deal and found local buyers for the team. Almost immediately, to establish credibility, the new owners signed Bonds and made Dusty Baker the manager. And a team that finished 72-90 the year before made an instant turnaround, wining 103 games and leading the NL West for much of the season. Unfortunately for San Francisco, its big year came in the same season that Atlanta won 104 to capture a third straight NL West crown.

The Atlanta-San Francisco race went down to the last day of the 1993 season and marked the end of pennant races as they have been known. Major league owners decided to realign the two leagues, creating three divisions in each and expanding the playoffs to eight teams.

The new divisions look this way:

EAST	CENTRAL	WEST
Baltimore	Chicago	California
Boston	Cleveland	Oakland
Detroit	Kansas City	Seattle
New York	Milwaukee	Texas
Toronto	Minnesota	

NATIONAL LEAGUE

EAST	CENTRAL	WEST
Atlanta	Chicago	Colorado
Florida	Cincinnati	Los Angeles
Montreal	Houston	San Francisco
New York	Pittsburgh	San Diego
Philadelphia	St. Louis	

New York Yankees owner George Steinbrenner autographing baseballs.

All of those moves were made without benefit of a commissioner. In an attack of geographical common sense, Fay Vincent proposed moving St. Louis and Chicago out of the NL East, swapping spots in the West with Cincinnati and Atlanta. It was one of several independent ideas that disturbed his bosses and ultimately caused them to lead Vincent to the exit. He resigned on Labor Day weekend 1992 and baseball was in no great hurry to replace him. The Executive Council ruled the game in 1993 with Bud Selig, owner of the Milwaukee Brewers, functioning as its chairman, a sort of commissioner pro tem. It was the first time in nearly three quarters of a century, since Kenesaw Mountain Landis, that baseball conducted its business without benefit of a commissioner.

As the sport headed for 1994, a new collective bargaining agreement was being negotiated and ownership was wrestling with proposals for revenue sharing that would allow small market teams to compete on a more equal footing with big city clubs. The $1 billion-plus bonanza television contract had expired, replaced by a less lucrative deal that would reduce income significantly. Still, the clubs still seemed to spend big money and in less than one week, Colorado, Texas, San Francisco and Baltimore invested $52.1 million to sign four free agents. The bulk of the money went in a $30 million deal Texas used to lure Will Clark away from the Giants.

That was nothing compared to the $280 million that teams spent on free agents in one frantic week at the 1992 winter meetings. A convention that once concentrated on trades has turned into an auction with agents, the new power brokers of the game, selling their clients to the highest bidder. That was the major reason baseball discontinued the meetings in 1993. The game though, hasn't yet found a way to discontinue the big money contracts.

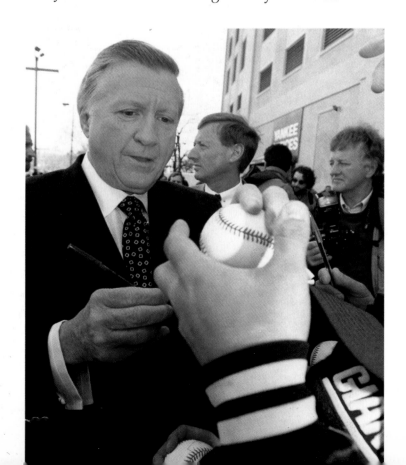